WITHDRAWN
FROM THE
PRATT INSTITUTE LIBRARY

You Don't Say

D0107309

You Don't Say

Modern American Inhibitions

Benjamin DeMott

With a new introduction by the author

Transaction Publishers
New Brunswick (U.S.A.) and London (U.K.)

PMC
973.92
D387

New material this edition copyright © 2002 by Transaction Publishers, New Brunswick, New Jersey. Originally published in 1966 by Harcourt, Brace & World, Inc.

All rights reserved under International and Pan-American Copyright Conventions. No part of this book may be reproduced or transmitted in any form or by any means, electronic or mechanical, including photocopy, recording, or any information storage and retrieval system, without prior permission in writing from the publisher. All inquiries should be addressed to Transaction Publishers, Rutgers—The State University, 35 Berrue Circle, Piscataway, New Jersey 08854-8042.

This book is printed on acid-free paper that meets the American National Standard for Permanence of Paper for Printed Library Materials.

Library of Congress Number: 2001054000
ISBN: 0-7658-0851-X
Printed in the United States of America

Library of Congress Cataloging-in-Publication Data

DeMott, Benjamin, 1924-
    You don't say : modern American inhibitions / Benjamin DeMott ; with a new introduction by the author.
        p. cm.— (Classics in communication and mass culture series)
    Originally published: New York : Harcourt, Brace & World, [1966].
    ISBN 0-7658-0851-X (pbk. : alk. paper)
    1. United States—Civilization—1945- 2. United States—Social life and customs—1945-1970. 3. Inhibition. 4. Taboo—United States. I. Title. II. Series.

E169.12 .D44 2002
973.92—dc21   2001054000

For
Janet and Gerard DeMott

Contents

Contents

Introduction
to the
Transaction Edition

These essays were written in service—more or less—of a single theme, namely that nothing is as simple as it looks. They're no good for dozing. At one moment a piece appears to belong to the political or cultural left, at the next it appears to belong to the political or cultural right, at the next it's headed somewhere beyond. Elitist postures and mucker poses coexist from sentence to sentence. The writer identifies with a murderous assassin, a loving man of prayer, a youngster gripped by a fantasy of absolute freedom—which is to say, the writer's sympathy lacks decent limits. His apparent aim is to push hard enough for a grasp of what's out there to stir unease in readers about familiar perspectives and standard brand intellectual alliances. Putting the same point differently: the aim is to dramatize that thinking and imagining usually stops too soon, misses one or another moral, social or historical relation, is under ever slyer pressure to reduce, simplify, quit—and should, no matter what, resist the pressure.

This perceived situation—thought under pressure to stop too soon—doesn't change a lot from decade to decade. Today's morning's talk show (we are speaking of a morning in the summer of the year 2001) has a question for the "critic-at-large" of a mass weekly specializing in entertainment: How do you explain current enthusiasm for television programs that inflict pain and humiliation? There were many this season and reports say there will be many more next year and on into the future. Give us your thoughts, sir. Critic-at-large explains, in the brief sentence allowed, that the 18 to 49 demographic coveted by advertisers likes these programs because "young people like gross stuff and later they grow out of it." The short answer is appreciated, as are the short answers at presidential and other press conferences, as are truncated responses elsewhere. The latter habituate the world to pseudo-thought, gradually inducing belief that fullness of response is self-indulgent, vain, possibly even sick. To repeat: the pieces at hand were meant to say *No* to this belief.

They belong, obviously, to a moment when speaking out against the reductive impulse—treating that impulse as morally and politically destructive—did not yet require endless apologizing and self-justification. When exactly did this magical moment occur? Go by the calendar and it was forty-plus years ago. Go by essential history and the moment figures as the eve of the earthquake called "the Sixties." For completely non-mysterious reasons, *action* was very shortly to become the word. During and after the earthquake, a northern white liberal who cared about race injustice, say, had to go south to participate, however marginally, in the civil rights struggle; I myself obeyed that imperative.

But just before that time, in the period of this book's germination, a more detached, non-combatant stance remained an option that didn't inspire guilt; it seemed possible to speak sympathetically and still judgmentally, weighing the claims of the activists risking their skins day to day to effect change *and* the claims of those who deprecated the activists as self-deceived sentimentalists or squanderers of public funds. History itself could be brought into the equation: the report in *You Don't Say* about a Harlem volunteer schooling project under fire for "corruption" goes at some length into nineteenth-century diagnoses of the needs of "the disadvantaged"—diagnoses arrived at by the Abolitionists, subsequent critiques of those diagnoses by historians, and tangential matters. The purpose wasn't to evade judgment but to arrive at a judgment that takes account of how each part of a situation plays on every other part.

The same determination not to reduce—the same longing to be commensurate with whatever behavior is in view—turns up throughout these pages. A piece about *Playboy* connects that magazine's mocking presentmindedness with the mockery in high culture, over the past century, of "traditional values." But the analysis makes room for an account of the differences as well as the similarities between current mockers and their tutors, even for a footnote glance at past opinions from Dr. Johnson to Henry James on marriage and maternal feeling. A piece about new-style, irony-laced "contemporary" greeting cards spends much of its teasing space on the gap between these dark messages and the "gooey American innocence" in the greetings with which they compete ("Where the Old Greeter meant to represent himself as better than common men, the New Greeter means to be recognized as worse"). But before it's done, the piece spells out *likenesses* between these greeters ("both are hired stand-ins for the speechless") and traces a line of American inarticulateness from Myles Standish's friend to Joe Christmas, Prufrock, Coolidge, and beyond. A parachutist's wordless in-air experience, all action, gets a full page to itself and so, too, does an articulate jumper's attempt to name the pertinent freedoms ("You are the master, nothing holds you that comes from anywhere except in yourself"). But in time the book side of the aspirations enters, through the interpretive voices of J. S. Mill and Erik Erikson and the poet John Ashbery.

Always the writer is seen lobbying for broader views than those that shape first reactions. Yes, I say in "Dirty Words," the theme of Silence as virtue turns up everywhere in twentieth century literature, Conrad to Hemingway, Murdoch to Salinger. And yes, the theme has religious resonance. But can the theme really be understood if it's viewed purely as a sacrament, not as a strategy—a power ploy? Would such a theme have emerged had literacy remained the preserve solely of the empowered? The frustration of the elites in ages of mass literacy is easy to comprehend—but how should it be judged? The essay argues that no exemption religious or aesthetic can be granted to the thesis that language is the enemy of truth; criticism of the thesis based on political and moral standards is wholly appropriate.

Throughout *You Don't Say* praise goes to writers who turn subjects around—gaze at them from unfamiliar as well as familiar angles, aware that defects have virtues and vice versa. Praise also goes to those who are impatient with attempts to purify politics of social aspiration or delete vision from literary art. In spite of the risks of appearing under-outraged at McCarthyism, Richard Hofstadter honors the democratic undercurrent in American anti-intellectualism; in spite of the risks of appearing oblivious to the high cliché levels of key idioms in the language of the politics of hope, Arthur Schlesinger honors the content of old-style humanitarianism. Both writers are approved for their seemingly instinctive hostility to reductive modes of thought, and their suspicion of simplification.

My book strikes me in retrospect as, in a word, consistent.

This is, of course, a minor achievement, if achievement at all. The question that counts about any line of approach—or method or prejudice—is: What exactly can it produce?

My answer is that, on occasion, it produces sentiments and orientations for which a democratic and egalitarian-leaning society—hustling, down to earth, sentimental—can find serious uses. The signature feature of these sentiments—preoccupation with issues of hierarchy—reflects concerns that possess or deserve to possess great dignity and moment, given the inevitable tension in such a society between stated ideals and daily temptations. The effort to speak to those issues in relatively straightforward terms can't always avoid the traps of reductiveness I was just citing as the book's target. The assumption that virtually any contemporary cultural artifact and much contemporary behavior lends itself to examination as a sort of theater of the democratic dynamic can lead to layerings of analysis that imbalance a piece. As this suggests, ponderousness is always lurking and there's never enough humor.

Still the sentiments and orientations seem to me, as I said, useful. Whenever the rhetoric of equality claims to be more than rhetoric, it's sensible to look hard at those who exploit the rhetoric—managers, organizers and communicators—from the point of view of those they treat as inferiors. (Whether the managers side with or against the presumed inferiors is immaterial; illumination can occur either way.) Wherever fairness to all is represented as a cherished value, it's sensible to inquire into the insides of hidden, earned and unearned privilege, measuring the nature of the moral and political vulnerabilities to which both give rise. Wherever the gospels of democracy (mobility, self-realization, "development") are preached and revered, it's sensible to reckon their human costs as well as benefits.

Coming to cases: the piece in this book about *Playboy* pauses in its survey of that magazine's gestures *de haut en bas* to consider social postures taken up by other magazine successes of the period. It notes for example that, "for all the pleasant rural pathos of its covers, the shy egalitarian gentleness of its tone, and the passionate sentimentality of its embrace of Down East 'natives,' the *New Yorker* is an anti-pastoral; and, as it separates the slicker from the rube, touring Elmira or Dubuque for the pure comedy of Upstate or the Midlands, shrugging off the 'country' and national solidarity, it releases its audience from the wearing piety of the democratic ideal." And the piece adds that "for all its 'firm conservatism,' *Time* is uninterruptedly engaged in promoting disbelief in the different man, the larger talent, the holy genius." The aim of such observations is to freshen awareness of taken-for-granted *in*egalitarianism and leveling postures: habits of mind and expression which, without drawing attention to themselves, are constantly eroding ideal democratic understandings, attitudes and values, persuading us to regard those understandings as immature or outré.

Another piece reports on the decline of political parties in a Northeastern state, on the broader alienation of the populace from political concerns, and on the damage thereby done to the faith on which all effective protest against fast-fixed hierarchy rests: "As the long democratic struggle to replace suspicion of governors with confidence in them is given over, politics itself, the organization of *public* life, emerges as the ultimate unspeakable of human experience." A piece on anti-Americanism notices how that phenomenon functions not merely as a medium for expressing conventional repugnance at American vulgarity but, in addition, as a back door through which the hierarchical mind can reinsert itself into cultural life. The same holds for an essay about *ressentiment* as manifested in certain intellectual/academic fashions: "It is by no means fanciful to hold that most of the new academic enterprises of the humanities in this century—analytical philosophy, linguistics, semantics, the new techniques of literary criticism, the very emergence of literature [and deconstruction, one could add] as a study—owe their inception in part to the desire of the clerk to repossess himself of mystery, to take language out of the public domain, to give just desserts to an age in which everyman believes he owns and understands the word."

Even the reflections on African imaginative writing—the subsection of that writing that dares to utter negative words about "development"—become, at length, a disquisition on the contradictions and complexities of democratic consciousness:

> The young novelist of Nigeria . . . may well persuade many that the new alienation is worse than the old dispensation. But it is at least as likely that he will help to establish awareness that human problems survive social transformation, and thereby ease the enormous and inevitable disappointments which, in other over-expectant worlds, have led to violent reactionary rage. By protesting in the name of *his* feelings, he lays it forcefully down that the 'revolution of rising expectations' is a billion revolutions, numberless contradictory wellings of perversity, passion, industry, and sloth which, because inward and personal, cannot ever be fully comprehended in the flat public language of success and failure. And to possess this knowledge is to possess precisely that human consciousness, clear, complex, unillusioned, which is the ideal destination of the ascent.

Not on many pages of *You Don't Say* are the basic issues and problems of democratic life—the temptation to broker off the aspirations and challenges and frustrations for what's happier, more relaxing, less demanding—out of sight.

A word about the "circumstances of composition." The germinating time for these pieces was the late Fifties. I was an English teacher (a Ph.D. in literature), and my first publication, using the term then going in the academy, had been a short story in *Partisan Review* in 1951. I wrote more stories throughout the Fifties and a novel of mine came out in 1959, and another novel later on, but I had impulses better suited to longish essays than to fiction. I wrote book reviews for various literary magazines, and at length I proposed to the editors of *Commentary*, for whom I'd done several book pieces, a reportorial essay on "intelligence in Washington." I was offered a small expense account and large encouragement.

The piece appeared, drew some notice, and produced an offer from Hiram Haydn, a Harcourt, Brace editor, to write a quarterly column for the *American Scholar*, the Phi Beta Kappa journal that he also edited. The column, called "An Unprofessional Eye," ran regularly, and five of the pieces became the nucleus of this book. About a year or so into the column's run, during a hotel breakfast in Manhattan, Haydn asked about my book ideas if any. Most of what I had been working on lately, I told him, seemed to be about inhibitions—contemporary inhibitions in a reputedly inhibitionless age. Drawn together, these pieces might make a coherent work.

My editor liked the idea: "Send it and we'll do it." And he and Harcourt did exactly as he said.

What's omitted from the foregoing account is the uncertainty each step of the way. I had a scholar's degree in a specific academic field (English Literature, 1660-1750). Aside from a few monographs culled from a doctoral thesis, I was ignoring this "specialty," therefore my "career." My first column in the *Scholar* consisted of an on-the-spot report on the trial of Norman Mailer for a knife attack on his wife—a step removed from critical essays on Dryden and Pope. When an optimist friend in a high place at a Great University put me up for a nice job at that institution, one of his colleagues circulated my piece on *Playboy* throughout the Great University's English Department, as evidence of my turpitude. Blackballed. Serious commentary on popular culture appeared regularly abroad, but not here.

Beyond this lay the complexity problem, a.k.a. the obscurity problem. If what one was after was commensurateness, one hadn't a prayer of reaching an audience large enough to support fantasies of earning a living by writing. (I was a World War II veteran, married with children.) And, to carry the story a little deeper into the Sixties, if one was hostile to reductive rhetoric and expressed that hostility in commentary on extravagances in the peace movement, one got knocked around as a Tory, a warmonger, or worse. In the middle two decades of my writing life I functioned mainly as a reviewer, lucky to get into print.

Why call to mind these half-forgotten vicissitudes and dark hours? Not in order to avow that my humblers and humiliators were way wrong. Over the last forty years the idea of the "literary scholar" has taken terrible hits and lost much vigor; the preservers of the tradition who guarded the Great University gates against the barbarian me are now cold in their graves, but they soldiered in an honorable cause. As for my sacred vision of commensurateness: the Pentagon papers stove in my confidence in it, forced me to acknowledge what my brighter brothers and sisters knew years before: the authorities can seldom be trusted even half way and a scream can sometimes be the only means of uttering the truth that the babble of moderacy engulfs.

No, I'm actually not on this subject of past troubles for purposes of self-justification. Conceivably young writers in or out of academe who have a notion of what intellectual journalism should be and currently isn't—or a fresh concept of what the worn phrase "public intellectual" ought to mean—won't be harmed by hearing a few sentences about how one such "career" went in the middle of the last century: what sort of scrambling it entailed even if you had a job, how often an assigned piece wound up back on your desk (no clear reasons given), how journals that couldn't get enough of your work this year forgot your number the following year and for three decades or so thereafter, what it felt like to learn that your "style" was "ripped apart" by gifted rippers at department meetings of the Great University, etc. etc. I believe it's easier now than it was then to travel the route I chose, and, if so, my purpose in running on about the past would be, of course, to lay a claim that people like myself ought to get a pat for making it easier.

But in fact, none of the above. I have perfect clarity about my reason for looking backward. It's to do with desire to revisit a particular moment of joy in its context—a moment half-forgotten, incredibly, until the reissue of this book was broached. I remember I was in New York on writing business and a Harcourt publicity person asked if I had seen "your wonderful review in the *Times*?" I read the thing through hastily in the Hippodrome garage, waiting for my car. A cursory uncomprehending reading, performed by the travel-mind: the getting out of the city Friday afternoon mind.

Outside the city I pulled in at the first Turnpike rest area and reread my "wonderful review." The piece was by a critic named R. V. Cassill, not known to but respected by me. There was a photo of my map in the middle of the page—mouth silly-wide with laughter. I'd never seen it before. The praise ran paragraph after paragraph, the word "intelligence" clanging in headline and text.

In domestic life and through the lives of my children I've learned much about joy. I know, moreover, that people who are hugely moved—whether exhilarated or depressed—by the judgments of others on their performances suffer from a dependency that is, in itself, very bad luck. The other week (we are back in 2001), in the same reviewing medium in which R. V. Cassill cried me up almost forty years ago, a young writer saluted my latest book as "hopelessly out of touch." And because I'm a relatively lucky man, the wound is healing nicely.

On the other hand, one solid memory of the surprise of fullthroated praise survives and still stands well beyond price or valuing. Even half-forgotten it does not wither. I remember the place and hour of exultation perfectly. I remember shouting at myself, "Ben! Ben, *ba*by!" I remember banging the steering wheel with both hands and wanting it to dance with me. I had been writing for close to twenty years, counting the earliest mishaps, and had never heard praise unsmutched by reservations about my "difficulty," "obscurity," "over-literary approach," "Jamesian diction," endless sins. And all at once it was over. Amazingly, inexplicably, at some rest stop in Connecticut: you *win*. How? What happened?

It comes back, as I say, perfectly clearly—the sudden nourishing change from the dreary, dreary weather of reservation. Not possible to forget.

Let me add that I remember Hiram Haydn with warm gratitude, and that I am very fond of *You Don't Say*, and that, for me, it's a delight beyond ready measure to see the book back in print.

July 2001
Worthington, MA

Foreword

The pieces collected here harp on a simple truth: certain ways of feeling and talking that once were perfectly acceptable are now, in effect, forbidden. It is a truth that turns up often in sermons on the vanity and self-deception of modern men. Conservative sages, for instance, cite the disappearance of traditional styles of expression (patriotic, religious, moral) as evidence that the present self-congratulating age of liberation is actually repressive as hell. Modern man *claims* to have conquered inhibition, say these critics; he claims to have advanced beyond stupid restraints and pruderies. But the fact is, inhibitions are endless—the late twentieth century like every other age has taboos, dirty words, and repressions, and it is senseless to believe that some promised utopia ahead will ever release anybody from the intellectual captivity of man.

There is of course a sliver of substance in the argument
that the age of liberation has proscribed some areas of
thought and feeling. Direct statements of positive feeling
—loyalty, love, admiration for another—are at the moment considered bad form. The language of idealistic service is in disrepute, and personal ambition has itself become
nearly inexpressible. In public areas of discourse the word
politics is regarded by many as an obscenity, and decent
circles no longer tolerate the phrase *democratic ideal* or
allusions of any kind to the moral strength of a society
unstructured by class. And in the world of high culture,
the fashionable enthusiasm for Silence as a supreme human
value seems now to be creating distrust of every expression
of sequential reasoning.

But a sliver of substance isn't enough to build sermons
on—and, to repeat, people who are upset about modern
muteness do tend to preach. Dr. Jeremiah Stamler, director of the Heart Disease Control program of the Chicago
Board of Health, remarked recently that he knows young
men who say, " 'If I put on this application for education,
"I want to better human health," people will think I'm
faking. People just don't talk that way.' " Stamler spoke
sternly against the inhibition, insisting that "if people
really feel this way [committed, that is, to a high purpose],
they should state it." But why assume the inhibition in
question is valueless? Is it true that perversity alone and
a silly fear of sentimentality—the "meanest of modern
terrors," as G. K. Chesterton called it—are the forces that
cause students to clam up? The language of unselfish commitment was raided and degraded long ago by PR types,
copy writers, image builders—men who make slugs out

of every term they touch. And it is therefore quite possible that students who object to that language do so in
order to assert their moral dignity and intelligence.

Nor do the ambiguities attending verbal commitment
and its opposite end here. "Thought is deeper than all
speech,/Feeling deeper than all thought"—William James
liked to quote these verses to warn himself and others
about the limited powers of language. And an awakened
consciousness of the limits of language can mark an intellectual step forward, even though the immediate result
of the progress is to choke off some avowal of hope or
solidarity. A year or so ago Charlayne Hunter, the first
Negro girl to enter the University of Georgia, told a *Time*
reporter that her public appearances before civil-rights
groups made her feel "like a hypocrite . . . all that *We
Shall Overcome* business. . . ." Adding quickly that "I
believe in it, sure—" Miss Hunter explained that "there
are some things I believe in that I just don't believe in talking about." And her quandary, her awakened need to dissociate herself from the conventional language of a cause,
was very likely a growing point in her personal experience.
Again and again in the past, self-imposed acts of censorship, refusals to utter the accepted inspirational word, have
proved to be acts of public service, signs of the achievement of a confidently individual intelligence. (For con-
firmation, see the essays in this book about radical African
writers, and about daily life in a totalitarian state.)

What is needed, in short, isn't another high-minded call
for the grand old words, or another warmhearted threnody
on the hearth and flag. Neither is it a new puff for progressivism with *its* simplistic rhetoric about calling spades

spades. The curse of the modernist or liberal line about inhibition and repression is obliviousness to major lessons of contemporary thought—in particular, the lesson that ideals and facts, myths and physical laws, aren't in combat with each other, but are supplementary and mutually limiting versions of reality. (What this means, to give an unpretty example, is that lamer-brained modernists unconsciously link phrases like *to fuck* with truth, science, and the end of the Dark Ages, while phrases like *to love* are associated with deceit, superstition, and "fairy tales.")

All that can possibly help at the moment is a flexible, complicated—and humorous—understanding of the meaning and bearings of inhibition. A person possessing such understanding concedes that while muteness and bad oratory can be equally mindless, the former does less dishonor to an ideal than the latter. He accepts the necessity for skepticism of abstractions, and for wariness of lax, opportunistic manipulation of the language of value. But he refuses to concede that mere avoidance of that language, or habitual mockery of it, can meet the need for satisfactory terms of self-definition—terms for the expression of feeling and for the expression of moral and political beliefs—sayable words by which knowledgeable men can live.

The separate tries at hand—some of them soberer than others—work toward the development of less rigid attitudes about inhibition and liberation than are now the rule. The methods they employ are various: journalistic, historical, sociological, critical, and (once or twice) novelistic. The same is true of the territory explored: the current languages of politics and higher education have a place, as well as the current language of love. And the order of the essays carries a comment on one man's idea of the connection between what he himself is and has been, and between what he does at his desk and what he sees outside—a comment that now and then shifts the focus a bit. But the aim of a decent adequacy to the facts remains constant. So too, the writer believes, does his certainty that a supple awareness of the effective censorship of the day can toughen resistance to cliché and stereotype, and is absolutely indispensable to the survival of sharp minds.

August 15, 1965
Amherst, Mass.

You Don't Say

The Anatomy of Playboy

At first glance the magazines—*Gent, Dude, Nugget, Playboy,* and the rest—seem about as remarkable as bananas in a fruit store.

The widely publicized key feature is a foldout naked babe. The conception, that of a hundred successful publications beginning with the *Spectator* and Sam Richardson's model *Letters,* calls for an editorial voice functioning as a guide for the innocent, a tutor in manners and desires. The finish is standard, high-gloss Formica-American. The lust for respectability (which translates to: eagerness for acceptance by media men in the big agencies) appears identical with that of old Holidays and new Posts (which means that the magazines are hospitable to what are called name writers). The career of the man who launched or relaunched the form is itself pure convention—one more

Lucky Larry tale, as it were, to be added to the annals of entrepreneurial ascent. Yet even after these and other reservations have been gravely meditated, the new girlie books remain hard to write off. They swim, all sleazy bikini voluptuousness, with fewer hake in their wake, to be sure, than many of the great whales of mass entertainment now wallowing in commentators' kens. But when placed in the context of recent publishing history, their emergence ranks as a major popcultural event.

If the case were otherwise, *Playboy, Gent,* and *Dude* would still retain some power to fascinate. For the conventions that mark the inner and outer story of these magazines, however familiar, are charged with a kind of transfiguring intensity—as though clichés hitherto shaped only in snow or Neoprene were at last being cast in brass. Consider for example the career of the founder of *Playboy.* A nineteen-year-old Chicagoan named Hugh Hefner comes out of the Army in 1946, studies psychology at the University of Illinois and Northwestern, sings with a student band, draws cartoons for the humor magazine, marries his high-school sweetheart, has two children, fails as a cartoonist, fails as a copy writer at *Esquire,* is divorced and flat on his hunkers by 1952—whereupon he has The Idea. He buys one-shot rights to a photograph of beauty bare (Marilyn Monroe), dummies up some pages of jokes and reprint material as a background for the display, sells ten thousand dollars' worth of stock in the "magazine" thus contrived. The production first appears in the winter of 1953, swiftly finds its audience (a million subscribers and two million dollars in advertising revenue by 1960)—and even as it is doing so the publisher branches out. He establishes big-city key clubs at which readers and non-readers are permitted, on payment of dues ranging from twenty-five to fifty dollars, to be served at tables (beneath photomurals of beauties bare) by waitresses called Bunnies: carefully chosen girls who wear plastic ears, satin diapers, heavy breasts, and rabbit tails. These ventures prosper in turn (over four and a half million dollars in receipts in 1961; one hundred thousand members in Chicago alone), the publisher builds himself a palace on the Near North Side to house sweet-life parties, watches unperturbed as imitators appear, reads about Hefner the "publishing giant" in the *Saturday Evening Post,* and gazes back at his lean past with the serene, public-service eye of the success who not only has it made, but who has, in fact, introduced a heightening element— early diversification—into a worn-out old conte of up-from-knavery.

Or, for another example of cliché irradiated, consider the girlie books' manner of playing their roles as guides to the naïve. Other publications teach, but—suspecting that mass audiences are phenomena begot by editorial flattery upon illiterate pride—do not openly declare themselves as teachers. Their gestures imply that all of us are all of you (Dr. Spock yields to his distinguished colleague, Mom). The girlie books, severer masters, yield to nobody. "Our philosophy," says the publisher of *Playboy* in his penthouse, "is that you [not we ourselves: we have arrived] should strive to get into the sophisticated upper crust. . . ." Moreover his letter columns (they may of course be housewritten) are filled with remarks in which the *Playboy* audience defines itself as doltish. (A voice from

Bellingham, Washington, congratulating the editors for a TV symposium, begins by saying: "This boob from the provinces was much intrigued . . . by your Panel.") And the letter columns of the magazine's competitors are if anything even more direct in their attempt to freeze readers in the attitudes of postulants—witness this characteristic letter to *Gent:*

I joined the service at the tender young age of 18. Now let's face it, for the most part, a guy up until he's 18 or so doesn't do much supper clubbing or any extensive dinner dating. . . . I've suddenly discovered I know next to nothing. . . . It pains me deeply that I should be considered a "boob" when once again I join the ranks of Joe Civilian. . . . Frankly I need help.

Further piquancies stem from the awkwardness of the girlie books' effort at manufacturing high style. Most mass magazines, as everyone knows, are correctly viewed not merely as teachers but as glamour factories. The function of the glossy-coated page, as of the images impressed upon it—rubies in refrigerators, diamonds on hubcaps, mink on mustard—is to chicify the homely object, lift it to the levels of elegance defined elsewhere in the magazine. *Playboy's* account of the upper levels is, naturally, conventional. Mercedes Benz is the cartoon car; the addresses of the "Clubs" are quite swell (5 E. 59 in New York, 727 Rue Iberville in New Orleans, De Sales St. near the Mayflower in Washington); many ads celebrate standard swank (Witty Bros., Beefeater); the gourmet talk is all squab, curried crab, and bearded frogs legs; and the travel sections tell of smart doings in Vila Franca de Xira. But a number of the homely objects that the glamour machine seeks to buff to the radiance of those just mentioned are very homely indeed, and the machine in consequence often labors under extreme strain. It brushes downward from Miss Rheingold and Chesterfields (normal cutoff points for magazines like the *New Yorker*) to Half and Half smoking tobacco and a men's cologne called Sweat. And the reader who is flung in a page from East Side tailors and English gin into this advertising netherworld can at least say for himself that he has had an amusing experience of marketing chaos.

For the cultural observer, though, the special interest of the periodicals in question depends not at all upon these samplings of chaos or pedagogical forthrightness or mid-century Algerism. The world of mass entertainment, like other worlds, has both a habitual life and cruces or high points; and although for a time the popculturist was uncertain how to distinguish the one from the other—how, that is, to separate mere occurrences (a season of Ben Casey, a mound of *McCall's*) from significant developments—criteria are beginning to emerge. The surest of these criteria appears to be that which defines a major popcultural event as *success in a declining medium,* or vice versa. And the girlie books plainly qualify as events when judged by this standard. The past decade, as is well known, was catastrophic for mass magazines. Between 1950 and 1960 thirty-two of the country's two hundred and fifty largest publications quit the game—or merged. And as Woodrow Wirsig, editor of *Printer's Ink,* points out in

Harper's, "of the magazines reporting their profit and loss statements in 1960, 39 percent showed losses."* Aware of these statistics, no one can shuffle away the success of the girlie books into an easy generalization about rising literacy rates or normal patterns of production and consumption. Vulgar or dull, shy or brash, U or non-U, these magazines stand as counterthrusts to current reading trends, manifestations of a free impulse of public taste. And it is for this reason that their claim to regard, as puzzles worth more than a moment's effort to solve, cannot be dismissed out of hand.

As might be guessed, the key to the puzzle lies in the nature of the magazines' simplification of experience. The *Playboy* world is first and last an achievement in abstraction: history, politics, art, ordinary social relations, religion, families, nature, vanity, love, a thousand other items that presumably complicate both the inward and outward lives of human beings—all have been emptied from it. In place of the citizen with a vote to cast or a job to do or a book to study or a god to worship, the editors offer a vision of the whole man reduced to his private parts. Out of the center of this being spring the only substantial realities—sexual need and sexual deprivation.

From one point of view this particular reduction appears an accomplishment requiring little ingenuity. It is known that, just as great fear (in a foxhole) overwhelms

* The tale of disaster can be sketched too boldly: *TV Guide* emerged in this period, and, as Wirsig himself noted, magazine cirulation in the fifties grew substantially in educated, upper-income households. But it remains true that the magazines experiencing this growth were either elite (or pseudo-elite) publications which do not expect to achieve subscription lists in the millions, or (as in the case of *TVG*) productions riding the antennae of a different medium.

the forces that divert people from faith, so great heat (in a period of rut) overwhelms the forces that divert people from sexual absorption. And from this it follows that to simplify both people and situations you have only to induce heat—an easy task for any photographer or writer. There is, however, one strong locus of resistance to the idea of experience as pure fornication (actual or potential). Alone in his chambers a reader may believe that the world is his erection, but on the thoroughfare or in the office or in a back seat he has encountered conflicting testimony—someone's obliviousness to his need, a moment of rebuff, suffusion of shame. Between the hand on the paper Playmate and total acceptance of fornication as the World-Soul falls, in fine, the shadow of memory. And it is to the struggle against this shadow, the effort to block out the collective memory of incompleted passes, that the girlie books summon their full resources of deviousness.

The campaign, to call it that, strikes in several directions, but its main force goes to an attack on the notion that, for women, reluctance is the norm and eagerness the exception. *I* burn, memory says, but perhaps they do not. The magazines say: nonsense, they are always burning, are mad for it, have got to have it, are wild wild wild to be snatch. The chief exhibit in substantiation of the claim is of course the foldout naked babe. Wherever she is (Oslo, Rome, Nassau, Rio), whatever her occupation (ice-skating, skin diving, motorcycling, scratching her toes, aquaplaning, trap drumming), her eyes say: Oh please *please* give it to me now. And these eyes, these begging burning empty hands, are not to be dismissed as exotica. In a dozen canny ways the magazines undertake to establish that the nude in Nassau and the stenotypist in Schenectady —the sexbomb and the "ordinary girl"—are actually one creature: Essential Woman. The correspondence columns are filled with relaxed expressions of interest or opinion from "working gals"—proof that the girlie books' sense of experience appears sound to the Average Woman. Male correspondents apply the descriptive jargon of the magazines to their own experience ("Now that I have a Bunny of my own . . .")—proof that the *Playboy* characterization of women nicely fits the facts of commonplace works and days. More important, the magazines are at pains to demonstrate that their artistes are figures chosen from "all walks of life," not simply from burlesque runways (one form-shower, Miss Cynthia Maddox, is described as a receptionist; another, Miss Janet Pilgrim, is described as *Playboy*'s subscription manager and chief of "Reader Service"). Occasionally a breakdown occurs. The December '61 issue of *Gent* carried a letter from "Mr. Erwin Fuchs" of Passaic, New Jersey, inquiring whether the real name of an artiste featured in an earlier issue wasn't "Jeanette Camille Swanson who used to be a stripper and appeared at Minsky's in Newark. . . ." (The editor in his answer evaded the question.) But queries of this sort are excluded from most issues, and the pretense is firmly kept up: the desperate gaze is the gaze of Everywoman; she, they, all are at one with you, reader, in need.

And how overpowering, how maddeningly intense is this need! In the joke columns the pressure is lightened a trifle; the lecherous woman is gently teased (". . . the legal secretary who told her amorous boyfriend 'Stop and/or I'll slap your face' "; "Our Unabashed Dictionary defines assault as what every woman likes to be taken with a grain of"). And since the photographs speak for themselves, the cutlines beneath them venture little more than a suggestion, say, that the subject prefers copulation to conversation. (About bare-breasted "willowy Marya Carter," for example, the patient editorial voice of *Playboy* observes only that she works hard at "thesping studies, relaxes with the many boat-swains who find her a ship shape date to remember [though quick to put the damper on overly opinionated types who talk at length, she gets along swimmingly with more considerate types]. . . .") But the plain-text portions of the magazines are ridden page on page by the theme of female lust. Dozens of "ribald classics," chosen for the force of their dramatization of the appetites of women, are dragged out of the past into the glossy pages. *Gent* offers paraphrases of *Fanny Hill* in support of a redefinition of female innocence as a condition of intense orgiastic expectation. *Playboy* serializes the sad, sex-ridden sagas of Françoise Sagan for the purpose of proving that the Litry Lady herself, the big-money-high-class-sports-car Intellectual, has "nothing else on her mind." Even the casual spot drawing is placed in service of the effort to create the ferocious female Urge as supreme reality. The white space on a page of a recent *Playboy* was dressed with sketches of a man shaving with an electric razor, in the company of a Miss Buxom clad in black stockings and gloves. In the first panel the girl studies the wall plug to which the razor is attached; the second shows her pulling the plug from the wall—the man still shaves, owing to the current she generates.

Mere assertions of female sexuality, like those just cited, announce the existence of a common need, imply that rebuff is the exceptional rather than the normal experience—but of course this in itself hardly suffices to quiet every misgiving. Granted that if my pass had been made at another girl, it might have succeeded, why did it fail on the occasion I remember? If fornication is all, whence came the resistance that embarrassed me? The threat to a closed sex-driven world implicit in such questions is evident. Belief in the primacy of the needs and interests of individual playboys and girls can be sustained only as long as no competing interests are defined; one touch of the superego, one breath of the common air, one allusion to either social disapproval of promiscuity or moral approval of procreation and the reader is thrown back from the beguiling simplicity of sex fantasy into the tearing thickets of ordinary life. Despite the challenge, however, despite the apparent impossibility of rationalizing resistance without alluding directly to the demands and interests of society, the girlie books manage to face up to the threatening questions without in any serious sense smutching their pure, constructed world.

The modes of address to these questions are two in number. In the first, resistance is treated lightly, understood as part of a game called Appearances and Proprieties. As is obvious, there is a measure of daring in the admission of these terms to print; in common usage both words imply a social will that exists outdoors, beyond the isolated self, in a garden dense with spiky symbols of restraint and domesticity—cops, ministers, house detectives, Mann Acts, actions for non-support, double-ring ceremonies, dishwashing, PTA meetings, and the like. In the girlie books, however, none of these ominous suggestions appear. Appearances and Proprieties are defined—in stories, cartoons, even in layouts of bachelor quarters—as handmaids to delectation. They are no more to be condemned as evidence of social hypocrisy than are the statutes which prohibit catchers from dropping third strikes: they simply add touches of pleasurable intrigue to intimacy. The magazines acknowledge that styles of play vary in this game; they concede too that sticklers for rules may indeed *look* very uncooperative; and they take sober account of letters like the following (from "B. B." of New York):

Recently I asked a young lady of my acquaintance if she would care to spend a weekend with me in Las Vegas. She seemed delighted at the idea, and replied that she would be more than happy to be my guest. Then, after I had bought a pair of plane tickets and was about to telegraph for a room reservation, she advised me that, of course, it was going to be separate quarters. I now regret having asked her—but I don't know how to back out gracefully. What would be a suitable course of action in a situation such as this?

But in answering such letters the magazines do not even glance at the possibility that the weight of some impersonal law or convention may stand behind the young lady's position. "Honor your word and go," writes the "Playboy Advisor" to "B. B.," restating the view that concern about proprieties amounts to proof of availability. ". . . Her acceptance of the invitation and her insistence on the proprieties of separate accommodations imply a desire to maintain appearances coupled with a tacit will-ingness to be persuaded once you're on the scene."

In the second mode of address to the question How is a man to understand rebuff?, feminine reluctance is treated seriously—as sin. The argument here is quick-shifting and complex, to be sure. The magazines' primary principles are those which maintain the equality of sexual need and the relative triviality of most girlish hesitation. But there are secondary principles, introduced both to accommodate the more stubborn doubts and to add dra-matic tension to the constructed world (dullness con-ceivably could be the issue of a perpetual coincidence of rut and oestrus). And these principles acknowledge the reality of individual crimes, individual constraint. The key word once again *is* individual. The workings of evil, as traceable in the psyche of the seriously reluctant girl, aren't to be understood in light of social directives or in-stitutions, they are rather to be seen as the consequence of personal failings: the girl has limited self-knowledge, or is sentimental, power-mad, or greedy. The last motive, greed, is most often cited as the moral disease of which re-luctance is the symptom. Sallies at the gold digger range from clumsy aphorisms ("Year in and year out . . . the most popular [color] among women remains long green") to heavy jokes like the following:

. . . an aging and wealthy man-about-town . . . dates only the most beautiful girls and confides to each of them that he suffers from a heart condition (not true). Then he takes them home to his magnificent estate, where they are properly daz-zled by the quantity and quality of his possessions. He hints at the vast extent of his fortune. Then comes the clincher: he tells each wide-eyed, open-mouthed girl that, by the terms of his will, all his money and possessions go to whomever is with him at the time of his death. Then, so he claims, the girl usually does her level best to kill him with kindness.

And similar hostility crops out frequently in fiction. (A recent tale by a writer named Ken Purdy centers on a beautiful clairvoyant who uses her gifts to gull a wary millionaire into marriage. The girl has a vision of herself, shortly after the marriage, in the act of murdering her husband for being unfaithful to her. She describes the vision to her husband, and he responds with a proposal that they separate; the story ends with her answer, a fierce, dollar-crossed *No.*)

But some attention is also paid to other moral ailments —with the incidental result of a gain in literary variety. An essay by Alfred Kazin abusing "The Cult of Love" is admitted to *Playboy*—because the essayist's critique of people who believe in the possibility of a perpetually loving connection between two human beings has the effect of putting down the Bad Woman who cannot bear to confront her essential animality. A forum on the "galloping womanization" of America featuring intelligent praise of the second sex by Ashley Montagu and others is tolerated—because the voice of the editor has the first and last word, a speech against marriage ("the source of an aggressively domineering womanhood").

As these examples indicate, the effort to equate reluctance with individual sin sometimes leads the girlie books in the direction of misogyny. There are occasional stories in which fornication is treated as a chore. (One story tells of a rich, indulgent father who helps his son win the girl of his choice in face of the disapproval of the girl's detestably ugly mother; the service performed by the father is that of fornicating with the prospective mother-in-law, in order to persuade her to think well of him and therefore of his son, her daughter's suitor.) And adumbrations of the theme of the holy marriage of males are not infrequent. But these themes rarely dominate a whole issue of any of the magazines. They amount only to a kind of epicycle, as it were, a corrective adjustment insuring the perfect rounding off of the greater argument. The latter can be summarized as follows: The world is a collection of individual human beings each burning with sexual need. Evil exists—in the form of personal, pathological motives that lead certain individuals to face away from the truth of their need. But Good also exists—free copulation undertaken in accordance with Appearances and Proprieties, rules which (properly considered) increase the pleasure of the act rather in the way that nets on tennis courts increase the pleasure of tennis players. And, in the grand reckoning of experience, the victories of Good greatly outnumber the victories of Evil.

For the popculturist not the least interesting aspect of this version of experience is its point of connection with the versions developed in some notable magazine successes of recent times. The girlie books, in contriving a closed, abstract world driven by inward heat, banish a number of traditional ideals or values—as, for example, belief in the possibility that love is not a racket, or in the theory of fidelity as a virtue, or in a relationship between femininity and goodness (the good woman is an animal in heat, like the good man); they free their readers from an old burden—nagging intuitions of consecration, forced acknowledgments of a higher, sanctified object. And precisely the same observation can be made about such periodicals as the *New Yorker* and the Luce string, which are, at bottom, enormously successful enterprises at reduction. For all the pleasant rural pathos of its covers, the shy egalitarian gentleness of its tone, and the passionate sentimentality of its embrace of Down East "natives," the *New Yorker* is an anti-pastoral; and, as it separates the slicker from the rube, touring Elmira and Dubuque for the pure comedy of Upstate or the Midlands, shrugging off the "country" and national solidarity, it releases its audience from the wearing piety of a democratic ideal. And for all its "firm conservatism," *Time* is uninterruptedly engaged in promoting disbelief in the different man, the larger talent, the holy genius. It seems reasonable to conclude from these examples, together with that of *Playboy,* that an important desideratum for a fresh magazine success in the present age is a sharply focused, infinitely manipulable hostility to some enervated piety: nothing less than this can simultaneously simplify modern experience while offering readers absolute assurances of their modernity.

But an evening with the girlie books not only leads to speculation about the elements governing the success or failure of mass magazines, it confirms certain guesses concerning popular understanding of modernity itself. Why, to ask the inevitable question, why is the present moment marked by extreme susceptibility to the *Playboy* fantasy— a societyless world in which ordinary ideals and standards are neither attacked nor mocked but simply "treated" as non-existent? The stock answer would speak of the "decay of values." The significant deficiency of the answer— as can be deduced from *Playboy* itself—is that the idea of decay does not accord with popular notions about the relation between Then and Now. The use of the word implies a present that is worn out, beaten by natural processes (erosion, mutability), too weak to believe as older generations believed. Whereas the sense of the present implicit in *Playboy* is fresh and liberated: people who share it might date the beginning of real knowledge close to the opening years of this century; probably tend to think of themselves as tough, clear-eyed, even heroically new; and doubtless are convinced that old orders are currently being rejected not because men are under-muscled but because men are impatient with the fatuity and superstition of ages past.

The point of moment here perhaps seems a shade more obvious than it is. Everyone knows that a recurrent gesture, or myth, in human history has been the myth of the fresh start: we here and now strip ourselves of old nonsense, here and now we make It new—both the individual (the American Adam) and the nation. And there is a connection between these gestures and the whole tone of the girlie books. But in earlier ages such gestures were complicated either by the desire to escape from history into the archetype, as Mircea Eliade explained, or by nostalgia —the feeling that, by scraping away the accumulated muck of certain periods of history, a man might put himself in contact with a favored, earlier epoch distinguished for its clarity and swiftness of perception. What is noteworthy about the popular modern gesture is that nothing complicates it: the substance of the past is understood as stupidity and self-deceit—murk dissipated, as it were, by a single giant (and undescribed) firestorm of the mind which, at an unspecified but recent date, had the effect of canceling every claim offered on behalf of previous rationalizations of society and value. The mind represented or created by *Playboy,* in short, locates decay in the past and understands the present as the first moment of intelligence for humankind.

Lectures on the limitations of this view are needless here. It is plain enough that the notion is science-ridden. Belief in cataclysms of the brain that smash every standing edifice can be justified where knowledge is considered to be a structure out there (a sum of learning to be mastered), where the act of finding out is thought to involve the replacement of one model by another, where inquiry is undertaken with full expectation of rapid obsolescence in the results. (Whitehead once remarked that before a discipline can become a science it must first lose its memory.) But humanistic knowledge, the goal of which is an alteration of inward being rather than mastery of outward fact, can only be thought of in these terms if the thinker accepts an excessively tendentious reading of the past.*

* A tendentious reading in that it seeks only the human absurdities of other ages—Werther, Eleanor of Aquitaine, Victoria on piano limbs, Keats's astonishment that women (perfect creatures) could "have cancers," Tennyson's engagement, etc. History developed in this fashion could make use of writers who claimed that fidelity was a virtue, and showed it forth unconsciously as a form of brutality or cloddish submission; it would ignore writers who in *their* recommendations of fidelity showed it forth as a mark of imagination (the imaginative apprehension of the pain one being can cause another

The sound reason for remarking the girlie books' dogma of modernity is simply that it stands as a convenient notation of the present state of relations between upper and lower culture. The tendency to consider old human conventions, vocabularies, and knowledge as matter to be scrapped hardly originated in mass magazines. For at least a century upper culture has been disposed to believe that any language which casts a light of ideal illumination or traditional moral significance over human relations, the connection of men and women, is a language no man of sense should allow to violate his tongue. The literary modes of adjustment to this conviction include the treatment of themes inexpressible in the rejected language—divorce in place of courtship, abortion in place of fruition, psychosis in place of initiation into social complexity. The novelist time and time again passes himself off as a thinker by offering lists of concepts—patriotism and courage, for example—which, like the phlogiston theory or the physiology of humors, have been "shown up" by the revolutionary new thought. The contemporary critic begins (as often as not) with a casual allusion to the probability that the thinking of the past on important subjects consists largely of lies. ("There are four things that people have habitually lied about: war, money, sex, and themselves," says Professor John Raleigh in a recent

---

by holding him or her lightly). It would preserve writers who understood love as a mighty transcendence of self; and omit all who understood love as a sum of gratitude to another for creating the conditions under which self-regard and self-acceptance become possible. Henry James's strong subtle letter in praise of his mother and of maternal feeling as a value, Dr. Johnson's remark that a man not married is only half a man—these and ten thousand other moments of unillusioned observation could be allowed no place.

Partisan Review, and he goes on to propose that ". . . war, money and sex can now be talked about with some degree of honesty. . . .") The painful philistine complaint that the new themes and assumptions of upper culture are mere morbidity fails to acknowledge the original goal of the inventors—an infusion of life and vibrancy into debilitated moral imaginations. And in pursuing this goal upper culture has for the most part avoided Wellsian crudities: it no longer asserts straight out that before the modern age people knew nothing worth knowing; it shies away from loud proclamations that "traditional values" have been supported only by stupidity (superstition, Mariolatry, absurd heroic romance), or by economic interest, or by stoicism (the Stoical Freudianism, for instance, that is incapable of taking in a Marcuse or Norman O. Brown). But on occasion its hesitancy about making such proclamations seems a mere tic of manners. And for unsubtle readers—people to whom the significance of tics is necessarily obscure: *i.e.,* the makers of lower culture— the oracular temptation to shock is irresistible.

Could the temptation have been indulged in the lower culture of the past? Certainly not, and here is one nub of the significant issue. The makers of lower culture until very recently congratulated themselves not for helping to realize the revolution against traditional values, but for helping to keep the old language up: they talked love, talked parental affection and obligation, talked the satisfactions of the good provider, talked the heroism of self-sacrifice in motherhood. Their language was debased, needless to say; disingenuousness alone can claim that the themes of forbearance treated in George Eliot have any direct connection with the lectures of Dr. Z. (in women's magazines) on problems of patience at the premenstrual turn of time.* And there is little virtue in the common insinuation that American upper culture was able to amuse itself (safely) with apocalyptic visions simply because public culture continued to celebrate old orders. But when these concessions are made, the truism remains: the world of culture was once sharply divided, high against low, in its sense of the worth of the moral inheritance.

And now the division is ending. The success of the girlie books is not the only item testifying to this turn of events (some notice could also be given to the sick western, the new humor, the abandonment of daytime soap opera, or even the announcement by the *Ladies' Home Journal* of its eagerness to print aberration tales and domestic fiction that "ends tragically"). But it *is* striking evidence: these magazines are without qualification postcataclysm, "through with all that," utterly sure that no existing moral language is adequate to modern experience ("Honor your word and go" because girls—not pledges—are made to be kept). Their single unironicized clarity (I burn, you burn, she burns, they burn) stands simultaneously as a motto for an emergent mass-cult school of kitsch existentialism, and as the ground theme for a whole new age—an age of Multiple Inexpressibles, a time in which *épater le bourgeois* will have become the standard *folk* gesture.

The task of criticizing such an age, to face at last the

---

* It is equally disingenuous, though (and more academic), to claim, out of worship of the aphorism about the inseparability of meaning and style, that lower culture is too vulgar in tone ever to be spoken of as capable of defending a value.

root problem, may at length seem insuperable. To repeat: the moralist who decides that the *Playboy* world is a projection of the elite, a contrivance reflecting the secret will of upper culture, ought to be condemned as a baiter of mind—a man unresponsive to the original need for a revivification of moral understanding. But this does not change the fact that the one language suitable for a direct critique of the girlie books is a dead language, and that upper culture was brilliantly in on its kill. The critical resource that remains—the aesthetic vocabulary (it permits an observer to cry Vulgarity!)—is perhaps not to be despised. Old writers, the third Earl of Shaftesbury for one, once sought to create a morality for aristocrats ("the grown youth of the polite world") out of it. But even in Shaftesbury's day, neither the polite nor any other world was polite enough to be ruled by an ethic of moral symmetry or taste. And at present those who use this language, in criticism of mass culture, achieve only an objectionably sniffish, unreal tone which brings to mind an image of Faubourg dandies praying on an A train.

The question, in sum (can there not be another language of assessment?), sticks hard; the slumming reader is uncomfortable in the act of evading it. Surely, surely, he mumbles, surely there is something more (an aspiration, a mind delighted in its powers, a father in tears at the thought of his child's pain, a wife in whose "tongue is kindness," whose clothing is "strength and honor"); surely "life does not come down to this," the coupling of beasts. There is something missing? . . . But where is it, what is it, how can it be fixed and known? Not through the agency of abstractions, says his fineness of response, his preference for the truth of drama as opposed to the truth of apothegm. Yet fineness, taste, adoration of tales instead of truthtellers, cannot possibly *place* the depravity of the stuff in hand: only the vocabulary of flat moral counters, which fineness scorns, can do that. The paradox implicit here may or may not serve as a fair, if indirect, measure of the vulnerabilities of an age of intense linguistic inhibition (about all plain terms save obscenities). But the chance is strong that hidden in its intricacies lies at least one of the stinking seeds that brought the girlie books to birth.

1962

The
Passionate
Mutes

If I could have but just one wish, this only would it be—
I'd like to be the sort of friend that you have been to me.

Old Greeting Card Text

When you leave it will be like part of us is missing—
. . . like a wart.

Contemporary Card

Ten years young, sassy, glossy, and hip, the Contemporary Card has suddenly become a smash.

Manufacturers reveal that sales of the item, once negligible, took a huge leap forward at the end of the fifties. Sharp-eyed periodicals like *Time, Newsweek,* and the *New York Times Magazine* are printing background essays on the product's early life. Publishers vie for the distinction of bringing out the first book-length collection of "classic"

CC's—a competition unprecedented in the annals of the greeting card. And the "editors" at Hallmark, and other original designers, have commenced writing self-congratulatory articles on their own achievement. The Greeting Card Association of America is a trifle wary, to be sure; its nervous press releases insist that the industry is still dedicated to the task of providing people with "emotional outlets . . . a sense of social well-being . . . a means through which friends and loved ones may express themselves easily and gracefully." But the voice of the trade association is ever that of the straight man—and not even a stationery straight man could suppress the startling tidings here. After almost a century of pastel paper lace and corny cantos, a revolution in felicitations has been launched—and the glory of its future seems assured.

To men of finance the health of the revolution is a weightier piece of good news than might be supposed. The manufacture of greeting cards is a three-hundred-million-dollar-a-year business. (The largest firm in the field turns an annual profit of from five to six million dollars, though it controls only about thirty percent of the market.) People by the tens of thousands earn their living from the trade. (Cards are sold in four countries by more than twenty-five thousand retailers, many of whom feature music by Muzak, "highly proficient personnel," endless racks of "Christmas Cards, All Holiday Cards, Special Occasion Cards, Religious Cards, Studio Cards, Contemporary Cards, Everyday Cards, Foreign Cards, Boxed Cards," and a setting free of such distractions as books.) Five and a half *billion* cards were sold last year, and responsible research has established that, after Christmas greetings are deducted from this total, an average of seven million cards are currently being chosen, bought, and mailed by American well-wishers every day of the year: to the expanding delight of everyone with a finger in the felicific pie.

Nor are money men alone in their pleasure. Audiences unimpressed by dazzles of digits and dollars nevertheless find special enticements in the emergence of the Contemporary Card. Aestheticians read significance into the replacement of old-style rippled papers, pallid colors, and curly calligraphy by sleek textures, brash blacks, and jagged type faces. And there is equally challenging matter for bookish folk. Admittedly the CC, when regarded as a literary form, does seem little more than a doodling in traditional modes. Its apparent satirical targets—Momism, Squareism, hypochondria, fortune-hunting, and the like—are familiar, and its rhythm (comparable to that of the double take or blackout) is unremarkably theatrical. On the front of the card—the opening scene of a skit, in a sense—appears a figure of good will; he smiles, utters, invites the reader to become one with him in simplicity, kindness, and sincerity. On the overleaf—scene two—stands a curt-voiced underground figure, leering at the front man and at every other gull. ("When you leave it will be like part of us is missing," says the smiler outside; "like a wart," adds the knife within. "If you tiptoe quietly over to the window and peek through the blinds, you just might see a group of young carolers in your yard," says the smiler outside; "stealing your hubcaps," says the knife within.) But actually neither mode, dramatic or satiric, is dominant in the Contemporary Card. Taken together the two "scenes" function as mockery of styles of speech, particular ways of talking—which is to say the CC's qualify, in strict terms, as parodies. As such they stand as the most complex literary productions ever to win a mass audience in America, and earn regard from literary types.

It is not, however, the vocabulary of the student of fine arts or finance that best defines the interest of the dialectic of the American greeting card. Like many ordinary purchases of luxuries and "expressions of taste," the choice of a card is correctly understood as a gesture of identification, a telling act of self-creation. The consumer who buys words is in effect borrowing a style—one that meets his need, suits his person (as he conceives his person), represents him better than any competing style, says what he "would have said" in the way he would have wished to say it. And, since part of any man's character is what he fancies "his character" to be, this borrowing serves as an index of a sort to the consumer's character. The value of such indices, even when they are available in a quantity of millions, can easily be exaggerated. Historians are reluctant to accept sales records of stationery salons as clues to the mystery of the modern temper, and trends in get-well cards can provide at most but a hint of an answer to great questions—as, for example, the question whether the twentieth century has finally broken up the Yankee archetype. But when the appropriate concessions are entered, it remains to be added that the development of greeting-card style over the years does possess piquancy for students of American character. Implicit in it, in the form of a guide to secret longings, is evidence about "character change" which, for all its rich unfinality, is suggestive—and surprising and affecting as well.

As might be guessed, the principal longing satisfied by the new-style card is that for the posture and airs of knowledgeability and world wisdom. And it is proper to admit that for the card-buying commonality this longing was almost impossible to slake before the advent of the CC. The voice of old-style greetings lacked subtlety; the self it created—guileless, optimistic, goodhearted, oblivious to the necessity of looking before and after, incapable of imagining an unamiable current in life—was a pure projection of yearnings for innocence. This self had enjoyed relaxing conversation with old friends—but had never suffered through an empty silence. ("If we could be together,/A little while today,/We'd sit and talk and visit,/And have such a lot to say.") It had met exuberance in new parents, but never anger or frustration. ("Just bet you're thrilled as you can be/Now that your family numbers three.") It had experienced "infant care" as ecstasy, but not as indignity. ("A baby in a bassinet,/A cuddly bear, a rattle/Two tiny arms that hug you tight,/The sound of infant's prattle./It all adds up to HAPPINESS/As anyone can see.") Even the concept of ups and downs—in, say, married life—had somehow failed to violate its mind:

Here's to the happy wedding you're remembering today,
And all those "big events" you've shared,
Together all the way.
—All those "little moments"
With a meaning all their own,

And, most of all,
The Happiness that both of you have known.

(The appearance of *all* as the key word in the old-card style testifies to the megalomaniacal tendencies of Innocence in the pre-revolutionary speaker.)

In the late or decadent years of the old style, a few dabblings in "awareness" could be noted. New parents were sometimes admitted to be busy ("You must have a lot to do/Since baby's come to live with you"). Praise was, at moments, set under mild restraints. ("What is a mother? A mother is a wonderful creature constructed almost entirely of love. . . .") And now and then the Innocent was allowed enough consciousness of inconsiderateness to plead for its remission. ("Been waiting for a letter from you./Any chance of one coming through?") But these were scarcely major modifications: the lapses into knowledge were brief, and the Old Greeter returned so swiftly to character that his delicate allusions to what Innocence mustn't know were virginal in quality. Rapt in a vision that included neither bodies nor boredom, he conveyed absolute assurance in the possibility of soaring upward from the plane of sin, death, feces, and guilt into the still white shimmering Allworld of love. And those who bought his words, perfervid Pelagians, were to a degree impersonating beatitude if not divinity: ascending magically from imperfection to the only state from which genuinely effective blessings have been known to come.

The alternative self created in the Contemporary Card (sales of about seven million a week) is a naughtier, rougher, and more masculine being, ill-disposed to flight, and, as the earlier observation about parody suggests, scornful of innocence. There is nothing the New Greeter does not know, nothing he cannot endure—but the man does despise illusion, and his manner betrays a determination, now perky in expression, now spiteful, to stamp it out. As a fallen creature, he has no truck with the notion that his largest debt to Woman is other than physical. ("I am 100% in favor of Mother's Day," he remarks in one card, "because just imagine where we would be without MOTHERS. Inconceivable.") He rejects the gospel of mother love, observing that many a mother would be delighted to part with her children. (A favorite CC text is: "Ladybug, ladybug, fly away home. Your house is on fire and your children will burn." The fire rages and the ladybug does not move.) His response to newborn children is topical and jocular rather than enthusiastic. ("POPULATION EXPLOSION," reads the headline on one congratulatory card. "Scientists say that if the present birth rate continues, in 600 years there will be about one square yard of land for each person on earth. You're not helping things any.") He confronts the myth of happy pregnancies with the fact of depression. ("Cheer up! ! !" says a card presumably suitable for "everyday" use. "My dog had the same symptoms last month and is just fine now . . . P.S. Would you like a free puppy?") And in place of the myth of the happy home, and the habit of filial deference, he sets images of generations and sexes at war. (". . . one must admit that Fathers at least try," says the caption on a Father's Day card. "Take yourself, for example; Mother often says you're one of the most TRY-

ING people she's ever known . . ." "Want to get rid of
that ugly fat?" asks the outline above a sketch of an obese
lady. "Divorce him!")

About matters of the romantic heart, the New Greeter
is equally rigorous—meaning he scraps the heart. Love in
his view is at best a matter of need ("I NEED YOU . . .
My psychiatrist says so"), and at worst a pratfall. ("Love
is where you find it," says the caption beneath a Valen-
tine's Day sketch of a girl digging in a garbage pit; "What
you're looking for doesn't even exist," is the comment on
the sketch of a forlorn, ugly maiden gazing yearningly at
the moon.) Between modesty and canniness in womankind
he sees no contest, bestowing his admiration forthrightly
upon the latter. ("A good man is hard to find," he remarks in a congratulatory engagement card, ". . . especially if you're a good woman.") His experience tells
him that the highest compliment to the legitimately af-
fianced is a suggestion that the bond formed is illicit.
("Just heard that at last you've found a perfect husband
. . . Now, if you can find one just like him that's single
. . .") He welcomes the rescinding of the old law that
forbade gentlemen to allude in writing to favors received
("We might as well be Valentines, we've been everything
else"). And he is certain that all the world loves—a
double-entendre ("I wish you two [newlyweds] would stop
long enough to let me wish you Happy Anniversary").

That the New Greeter's knowledgeability is usually dis-
played in the areas of domesticity and romance doesn't
signify that elsewhere he is naïve—or gentle-spoken. The
voice that utters in the new-style card knows that Santa
Claus is a bore. ("Season's Greetings, Dearie . . . Com-

ing to town this morning I ran into someone dressed up like Santa Claus. As far as I know, he's still there. Fortunately he didn't get my license number.") He knows that sick people need sallies not sympathy. ("Sorry to hear you're sick . . . I'd lend you my bedpan but I'm using it as a planter . . ."; *"Sick?* Don't worry. The death rate is the same as it's been for 100,000,000 years . . . one to a person.") He knows that almost anything can be turned into a joke. ("Where have you been keeping yourself?" says a caption beneath a photograph of Hitler.) And he knows that ambition and hard work are mere words. ("Your future is up to you!" announces a graduation card. "My millionaire uncle arrived in this country tired, hungry, sick, and without a penny in his pocket!! Fortunately he had fifty thousand bucks sewed in the lining of his coat.") And this miscellaneous savviness, like the New Greeter's shrewd views of marriage, the family, and the scheming woman, indeed like most of his wisdom, has its roots in the conviction that the gestures of sincerity are the gestures of madness—as the following "everyday" message obliquely demonstrates:

Somehow, this is the time of year when one's most innermost secrets must be told. With that thought in mind, well, the cloaks of modesty and shyness must be discarded . . . and, ah—you understand that this is quite difficult for me—but, yes, honesty is usually the best policy, even tho its use may make one appear to be a fool.

So with all this taken into account—and you know me well enough to realize that I am most serious and speak directly from my heart . . . well—please don't laugh, now . . . but . . . well . . . I think I saw Hitler yesterday.

The prime determinant of the man's character, however, isn't his unusual opinion about the nature of madness; it is, simply, his unusual aspiration—one that impels him toward the condition of sinner and cynic rather than toward that of saint. Where the Old Greeter meant to represent himself as better than common men, the New Greeter means to be recognized as worse. He wishes to be known as one who has journeyed past the world of love ("I'd like to be the sort of friend that you have been to me") and now stands poised at the grinning gates of perpetual suspicion ("If you're really going, there's only one thing left for us to do. Check the petty cash"). And it is this impulse, finally, this desire to pass oneself off as a soul besmutched into irony by life, that dominates the new felicitative style.

Since it is the New Greeter's difference from his predecessor that strikes the eye most forcibly, attempts at specifying his significance inevitably begin with formulas of change, transformation, and discontinuity. And, as might be assumed, numerous contexts for the application of these formulas are available. There is the sexual context, for one: the majority of card buyers are women, hence the emergence of a tougher voice can be presumed to reflect the new masculinity of American women. There is the context of social disintegration: given the increasing atomism of American society (the average family moves once every five years), a less committed idiom for the expression of social ties is surely essential for the preservation of emotional balance. In addition, there is the context of rising tension between the generations: the voice of mock respect in Father's Day/Mother's Day cards perhaps heralds the approach of the hour at which family continuities will vanish, and the land of democracy will indeed become, as predicted, a new country with every generation.

And then beyond all this lies the matter of shifting attitudes toward sentimentality: the exchange of the voice of innocence for that of experience could be regarded as evidence either of a new American maturity or of a resurgence of an old and admirable skepticism—that "basic mistrust of language itself" which, according to the late Leo Spitzer, is "one of the most genuine features of the Anglo-Saxon character." (Spitzer claimed that "in no language, so far as I know, are there so many prefixes which tend to unmask false values: *Pseudo, sham-, make-believe-, makeshift-, mock-, would-be-, fake-, phony-, semi-, near-* [beer], . . . *synthetic-,* etc.; it is as though the Anglo-Saxon attitude of distrust . . . would find for itself a grammatically fixed pattern of expression. . . .") If the Old Greeter was unafraid of sentimentality, he was also foolishly trustful of abstractions. Seeing, hearing, speaking only love, he saw no hatred, therefore no truth; his courage, to call it that, produced much nonsense in the American past; and the New Greeter plainly is in reaction against nonsense. The latter's style bespeaks shame at the gooey self-deceptions of American innocence (home sweet home, the endless frontier, truthful George, the Peace Ship, and the like). His will to ferret out the joke, whatever its hiding place, constitutes a rejection of lambent dullness as a value. And this in itself is nearly enough to justify talk of the Contemporary Card in which he appears as a break with the past.

But from none of this does it follow that the only reasonable account of the new style is that which stresses symbolisms of discontinuity and transformation. The New Greeter and the Old speak different tongues; the situations implicit in their texts (neighborhood farewells as opposed to office parties) are wholly dissimilar; neither man can approve the other's manners. Yet there are links between the two. The Old Greeter cries out: I am one who cares so deeply for your joy that the possibility of its being interrupted or troubled is intolerable to my imagination: I shall not permit it entrance to my mind, and perhaps the very firmness of my resistance will shield you from harm. The New Greeter cries out: I am one who cares so deeply for your joy that the possibility you will expect too much (of me or of life) and fall upon disappointment is intolerable to my imagination: I therefore set before you every obstacle, negation, hint of bestiality, vestige of Anti-Christ, evidence of Chaos: the better to guard you from obliviousness and disillusion. The Old Greeter stands forth as one part angel, possessed of access to the heavenly blessing and the heavenly comfort. The New Greeter stands forth as one part devil, possessed of access to the infernal knowledge and the infernal guile. But they are at one in greeterhood: maidenly or calloused, their hands do reach forth. And conceivably the gesture itself deserves regard as a Platonic idea—a message (*nothing ille come neare thee*) which in the world of ultimates cannot be altered by saccharine or by acid.

Is the latter notion a mere trick of levitation? Not at all. It is but a way of emphasizing that however different in capacity for feeling, or in intensity of belief in the magical powers of language, Old Greeter and New are indissolubly united in role: both are hired stand-ins for the speechless. The editors at Hallmark obscure this point in a preface to a house sampling of their work, when they attribute the "special vitality" of the CC to its concern "with what people do, say, and think right now." And character analysis of the kind offered here works to strengthen the impression that the voices in the cards are in fact real voices in real Edens (before or after). But obviously these are pseudo-, mock-, sham-, would-be-voices: not real ones. And to ignore this is to miss the most palpable (and homeliest) truth of the greeting-card dialectic—namely that, revolution or no, catatonia's still got the American tongue.

Nor is *still* in any sense an inappropriate term. The case is that the consumer of New Greetings is a man of tradition, as well as of revolt—a member, as it were, of the grand old army of passionate American mutes. The army in question is of a size commensurate with the land of Spokesmen-For, the nation whose primal chiding words of myth were: Speak for yourself, John. Sung heroes and unsung from every American century, Pelagians, Calvinists, pre-revolutionaries, post-revolutionaries, contemporaries, old fogies, Strether, Ahab, Dimmesdale, Christmas, Prufrock, Coolidge, even Mrs. Emily Post—all are of the company. ("Remember," said Mrs. Post's anxious chapter on the Personal Letter, "that every word of writing is immutable evidence for or against you, and words which are

thoughtlessly put on paper may exist a hundred years
hence.") Mired in universal quotation, caring too deeply
for tears and for words, generation upon generation of
Americans have heard the key turn in the door, have had
IT forever on (never off) the tips of their tongues, have
forever commanded what they could not give (You tell
me!—Say something!). Card buyers in any style are, in
sum, deeply in the American grain.

To say this isn't to deny that a revolution—a literary
revolution—has occurred, or that the naysaying style created is of use and moment. Richer for its new laughing
leering lingo, a mass audience has now the privilege of
mocking words it did not say with words it does not say—
and this game is a valuable distraction, releasing millions
from the torment of an unutterable affective life. It is to
assert, though, that here as elsewhere the cautious view of
breaks with the past is probably the soundest. Comes the
revolution, comes distraction—the style changes, the
words spin, the world swings. But when it is done we may
yet find in the open expectant doorway the Hi!-sounding
American still standing alone, full-eyed, wordless, all
*un*transformed:

> *Looking into the heart of light*
> *The Silence*

1963

Suspended
Youth

We escape
Down the cloud ladder, but the problem has not been solved.
John Ashbery

Sports event by billing, allegory in essence, the "Sixth World Parachuting Championship, Orange, Mass., USA" was pure farce in circumstance.

First announcements of the "attraction" appeared in the New England vacationtime calendar—a gatherum of broiler festivals and chautauquae in which the word *champion* points as often at potatoes as at athletes. Bad weather, which made chaos of the schedule of contests, and an impossibly complicated scoring system, which necessitated the use of digital computers, meant that spectators at the event were never clear whether they were cheering underdogs or front-runners. Efforts to dignify the competition by importing officialdom to observe it led to inelegant vaudeville turns. (A Member of the U.S. House of Representatives donned a parachute and leaped merrily from the guests' platform into the arms of some jumpers from Rumania—laughing dark-eyed women who accepted his embrace but fled from his French.) Efforts to encourage foreign competitors, whose hostel was a regional high school renamed "Friendship House," into intimacy with green hills and still valleys fell afoul of highway hazards. (A number of visitors went no farther than a neighboring Twist and Limbo Lounge, where they were caught in the strong toils of a belly dancer called Cashmere Bouquet.) The penultimate days of the event were scarred by a national defense alert, which grounded civilian aircraft and brought the competition to an abrupt unscheduled close, and by a sky-diving spectacular, produced by members of the U.S. Air Force parachuting team, which, though gravely described, drew chuckles even from non-purists. (In its feature, a "Duel in the Sky," free-falling jumpers dashed over the heavens before opening their chutes, firing Very pistols at each other and activating red and blue smoke grenades attached to their heels; the vivid air was signed with this *kitsch* long after the team's descent.) And the meet ended with a ludicrous, cold-war strike: jumpers in full gear mounted their planes for final leaps and then, sulking instead of jumping (while computers fumed), they rode idly about the skies—in protest against decisions seemingly prejudicial to the Czech and Russian teams.

To the money men who had underwritten the affair the fact of its commercial failure was, naturally, no joke. Optimists all, these figures had labored energetically from the start. Invitations to compete in the event were extended to dozens of countries by a "championship committee" whose advisers included Vice President Johnson, Governor Rockefeller, Senator Magnuson, Thomas J. Watson, Jr., and many other leaders of moment. (No fewer than twenty-four nations—Poland, Yugoslavia, Israel, India, Spain, Japan, and South Africa among them— sent teams.) A subsidy of a hundred thousand dollars was extracted from the state, which created a special commission to "assist in planning, promotion and development." Shepley Bullfinch Richardson & Abbott were retained to design a special "championship amphitheater." Townspeople in a dozen neighboring communities were pressed into service on housing, coordination, and "protocol" committees. The flow of notable visitors was constantly restimulated (a sample planeload from Washington included one major general, one naval captain, one USIS director of broadcasting service, three Congressmen, numberless aides, and a representative of the division of cultural affairs of the Department of State). And, at the appearance of the first signs of trouble at the gate, backers, officials, and competitors as well launched upon enterprises in public persuasion that were remarkable for intensity and inventiveness.

As might be guessed, not every claim made in the course of these undertakings was of the kind that wins instant assent. The "President" of the meet, a comparatively restrained booster, went no farther than to assert that it was "a revolutionary social step to have made the frontier of the sky available to the general public within reasonable limits of safety and expense." The "Executive

Director," disposed to an aesthetic line of appeal, avoided hysteria in presenting it. (Once, however, during the "Duel in the Sky," this gentleman seized a microphone and cried out to the sparse crowd: "Friends, free fall parachuting is an *art,* not a stunt!") And the series of announcers who stressed the significance of the competition as a venture in international palsmanship meant only to sound hospitable. (". . . the jumper now leaving Friendship Bowl is Evgenij Tkatchenko, what about a great hand for this great jumper from the USSR. . . .") But other voices were less reasonable. One member of the international panel of judges—Captain James Perry, of Fort Bragg, a trim young man on whose tattooed breast a covey of bluebirds was pinned in flight—sought to convince interviewers that sky diving was better regarded as a sound means of transportation than as an objectionable form of daredevilism ("It's like getting on a bus and going to work"). Reporters who talked with Mr. James Arender, a twenty-two-year-old Oklahoman who resembled James Dean, the late actor, and currently reigns as parachuting champion of the world, were persuaded that jumping improves a man's literary taste. "For relaxation," wrote an impressed correspondent for *Newsweek,* "Jim Arender likes to read Dostoyevski . . . discuss Voltaire." And Mr. Lewis Sanborn, Safety Officer for the event and among the most committed of the chuting zealots, defended the sport by arguing, first, that parachuting offered a way of teaching responsibility to delinquents (". . . you take these kids hanging around stoops and corners in the city, if they had a chance at this they'd learn what it means to be *responsible*"), and, second, that jumping experience helps to beef up bloodless businessmen ("executives who start parachuting become very aggressive in their line of work").

In these and other remarks of the principals there were hints of a drivenness that clearly deserved sympathy—but even those who extended sympathy stood more or less unmoved by the promoters' disappointment. In gambling and losing, the latter had at least bought the pleasure of a wager. And the competing teams, hurtling through individual and group events testing "accuracy" (in target landings) and "style" (in delayed-fall execution of turns, loops, back loops, and the like), were presumably competing for the joy of the contest rather than for the approbation of millions. The chief figure in the inner drama of Friendship Bowl was, in short, that of youth in the large, not that of the luckless entrepreneur or bookish champion. And while there was a moral lesson or two written in the red ink of the final ledger, the themes of the airy allegory mentioned were at once grander and more pathetic than any mere defeat of greed.

To say this isn't of course to write off as inconsequential every interest in a jumpers' meet save that of youth: techniques developed by sport parachutists have had military applications and may someday be of service to astral tourists. It is to say that the campaign to bring the event to America was a youth crusade. In recent years sport parachuting has enjoyed a small boom (city folk themselves have become fascinated, and a new jumpers' center opened this fall in New Jersey to "serve" them). But in the same period concern has mounted about the parachutist's image as a reckless scamp whose game of superlunary Chicken is offensive to public morals. Thousands of undergraduates and apprentices in the established professions (organized as the Parachute Club of America) were convinced that an international competition, drawing huge, interested crowds, not to speak of sportswriters hungry for copy, might banish the odor of the illicit that clings to the sport. And it was their enthusiasm (together with reports of attendance at meets held abroad—in Moscow, Sofia, St. Yan, France) that turned up the financial backing.

The intensity of the jumpers' concern about public relations is not entirely easy to fathom or, for that matter, to credit. On its face, the Parachute Club's estimate of the amount of hostility directed at its doings appeared extravagant—few citizens have felt constrained to work out clear positions concerning the merits of leaping from airplanes. Furthermore, in the psychological landscape of sport parachuting in general, worry and concern are not less evident than the familiar arrogance of the risk-taker, and the self-satisfaction of youth in possession of secret status. The adult world increasingly tends to define achievement in terms of "leisure activity," rather than in terms of labor or profession, and, aware of this, a young man whose recreation nicely separates him from the commonality would be refractory if he failed to admire himself. Yet this self-admiration, raised a power or two to arrogance, does decrease the impact of the parachutist's contention that worry about his image disturbs his rest.

Nor is there much in the outward life of a jumpers' airport that conveys an impression of youth taunted or oppressed. The artifacts of these Scenes—white Alfa-Romeos, black stretch pants, bleached goatees—are the standard stuff of modish, hipster sybaritism, and the air—in and out of the competing season—is the opposite of taut. Of an ordinary Sunday morning landing pits are rimmed with air mattresses on which visitors recline, scanning heaven for chute bursts, yellow, scarlet, green, and gold, and picnicking comfortably on whiskey sours and lobster rolls; roundabout autumnal hillsides church bells ring, but, as the smiling sons and daughters of Yale and Radcliffe suit up in their "Sport Sky Diving Sets," preparing for the joys of free fall, the public-address system teases the day with the un-urgent comping of Mr. Thelonius Monk, and the Puritan summons goes unheard. The tone of the foreign tents during the championship testified that this lazy-raffish, easy-riding youth style belongs to the whole jumping world, not simply to American chutists. In part the testimony was a matter of unities of gesture and posture: the pretty blonde *Fallschirmjägerin* from Austria took the sun in precisely the pose favored by the pretty blonde *parashyutistka* from Russia; the playful Rumanians who raced about shooting water pistols at each other, in parody of the "Duel in the Sky," slated the commercial gimmick in a spirit not wholly unlike that of the slogan chalked on the Aussies' tent—"The triangular chute is the best chute of all/For a very fine fall." In part it was a mere matter of the universal sameness of the apparatus of the suncult—lotion, dark glasses, bikinis, transistors, and the like. And the very internationality of the fun-house mode seemed to tell against the notion of the chutist as a harried man.

When all this is said, though, it has to be added that tolerance of sky diving is something less than a deep-rooted American tradition. The U.S. Government has not forbidden the game (a few European countries have done precisely that), but a number of governmental policies—as for example the ripping up of surplus chutes to prevent them from being sold for international parachuting—are regarded as essentially unfriendly, since they drive up the cost of equipment. (Parachutists are now conducting a write-your-Congressman campaign to alter such policies.) There are other signs—insurance restrictions, parental alarm, mass-media tsk-tsking—which indicate that the sport-jumper's chances of being left alone in the future are not improving. And, equally important as evidence that the un-anxious outward style is misleading, the comments of reflective jumpers betray, simultaneously, extreme wariness of disapproval, and an attachment to their pastime that is barely short of desperate.

The most obvious component of this attachment is, no doubt, the youthful need to reorganize relations between the self and otherness in a manner that will enhance the former and diminish the latter. Pressed for an account of his motives, the articulate jumper is likely to characterize the sport in terms suggesting that for him it amounts to a ritual of divestiture—a means of stripping off the layers of institutional lies and myths that encrust individual being. Often the truth of the impulse that first drives the jumper through the open door of the plane into hissing emptiness, in contempt of his most elemental fear, lies beyond expression—but for the current ecstasy words do exist. Free fall is free being, Man Diving is Man Alive at last. And from this it follows that the ecstasy is that of non-connection: the exhilaration of sinking the world to nothingness, or at least to stillness, and thereby creating the self as All.

The assumption of a parity between silence and mastery is in part a product of indoctrination. The *Sport Parachuting Basic Handbook* insists on stillness as a key value (". . . a peculiar silence settles around you . . . a total, strange silence. . . . The earth appears . . . more beautiful"). And, as already indicated, jumpers are often prodded out of their infatuation with formless freedom into contrived patterns of "flight." But again and again, interestingly, the competitors at Friendship Bowl expressed distaste for the restraining courses of loops and back loops through which they were forced to run. ("This formal thing—" said Miss Judy Simpson, a young alternate on the U.S. Women's team. "It's all wrong. The whole idea is just scrambling out, getting *loose*. . . .") And winners, losers, and tyros alike focused on the theme of self-liberation and enlargement. Mr. Arender likened his sensations to "what you feel when you're lying in a forest and you're all by yourself and there's only silence and the sun is going down. It's complete freedom in a world of nothingness." Mr. Bonno Wenkebach, a golden-skinned young "dental surgeon" from The Hague, likened his sensations to those of a polio victim entering the pool, feeling the weight of his braces leaving his limbs—a smooth assuaging flow of being. "You feel you are ceasing to be abnormal, tied up in irons," said Mr. Wenkebach. "You're

not controlled any more. You're normal instead—that's
the freedom of it. Freedom is what you *are*—no past, no
indirectness, apparatus. . . . You are the master, nothing holds you that comes from anywhere except in yourself." And, as he spoke, his less verbal teammates listened
with an approving soberness that itself attested to the
depth of jumperdom's involvement in the experience described, as well as to the intensity of its determination to
protect the sport from attack.

Appropriate historical and psychological contexts for
consideration of these intensities lie ready at hand. Lust
for unconditionedness or divestiture can be regarded as
one more symptom of what Mill long ago chose to describe
as "the age of transition"—a moment in history at which
people reject public definitions of the good or the free or
the normal, on the assumption that private judgment is
"the ultimate refuge, the last and only resource of humanity." (Mill's attitude, as will be remembered, was
stern: "Before I compliment a man or a generation upon
having gotten rid of their prejudices, I require to know
what they have substituted in lieu of them.") Or it can
be placed as an impulse attending psychological evolution,
and viewed with compassionate respect, after the manner
of Erik Erikson. Skeptical of rationalizations that appear
to endorse "any high-sounding self-delusion in youth, any
self-indulgence masquerading as devotion, or any righteous
excuse for blind destruction," the latter writer is nevertheless impatient with idle moralizing against the adolescent
flight from the given to the chosen. "From the middle of
the second decade," he contends, "the capacity to think

and the power to imagine reach beyond the persons and personalities in which youth can immerse itself so deeply," and as a consequence the young man not only wishes to be reborn "into a new reality," but to be "recognized as [an] individual who can be more than [he] seem[s] to be" —more than the mere conditioned, determined issue of history and family, core curriculum and freshman seminar. The effort to win this recognition may from the start be marked by a deviancy that is visibly devoted and indignant "in the service of a wholeness that is to be restored," and therefore easy for perceptive adults to value. But in other instances the effort may seem irresponsible and reckless— and this in itself is not proof of self-delusion:

. . . to some youths [Erikson writes] danger is a necessary ingredient of the experiment. Elemental things are dangerous; and if youth could not overcommit itself to danger, it could not commit itself to the survival of genuine values—one of the primary steering mechanisms of psychosocial evolution.

Considerations of the latter sort do much to illuminate the obscurer dimensions of the jumping game. But only when they are coupled with scrutiny of the metaphorical content of that game does light flow evenly on the sky diver as a symbol. Admittedly much of the content specified is unexciting—the parallel, for example, between youth (as a moment of suspension between the sanctuaries of childhood and adulthood) and free fall (as a moment of suspension between the sanctuaries of the plane and the canopy). Yet even this parallel gains a measure of interest when pondered. Youth's problem, as well-informed thousands have maintained, is that of determining when its suspension should end, when the claims of the world should be acknowledged. "The search for self which runs through the youth culture and the beat world," says Kenneth Keniston in *Daedalus,* "is not the whole of life, and to continue it indefinitely means usually renouncing attainments which have been traditionally part of the definition of a man or woman: intimacy and love for others; personal creativity in work, ideas, and children; and that fullness and roundedness of life which is ideally the reward of old age." But while the intelligent young man can agree that to continue the search "indefinitely" is foolish, he cannot say with much assurance when it is proper or sensible to cut it off. The society from whose imperfection and chaos he withdrew in dismay—perhaps in secondary school—is not markedly improved now that he is a B.A., or now that he has left the Army, or now that he has accepted a "meaningless" job drafting commercials or rockets: in none of these "forward steps" is there an imperative to *membership.* How and when will the imperative be felt? In what language will the summons from inward stillness to noisy human solidarity be uttered?

The absence of unambiguous answers is not wholly a misfortune. Human survival may well depend in large part upon the talent (political only in area of operation) for suspension, and years of uncertainty about where to Draw The Line may in themselves help to develop that talent. Yet the uncertainty is a torment; the young man enduring it is like the analysand debating within himself whether the moment has arrived at which to say: I am healed, my analysis is over, I am independent again. The words are sweet to the imagination—but who knows when to say them? who knows when his hour is at hand? One way of mastering the questions is by relocating them in a manageable environment and, oddly, this is what the parachutist has succeeded in doing. His apparently trivial game is actually an experience of suspension framed as a closed unit with a perfectly calculated, perfectly expressible beginning, middle, and end. At high altitude the sky diver leaps, within an instant he stabilizes his body, within twelve seconds the terms of his flight are fixed in numbers—one hundred and twenty miles per hour—by the counterforces of gravity and air resistance—and ever afterward his experience of freedom and nothingness, rolls and loops and scrambles, is a measured, scheduled experience. The clocklike face fastened to the reserve chute at his waist computes his future ticking, ticking, number after number naming the nearness of his approach to the Line beyond which lies a loss of bearing, a sprained or broken limb, risk of "malfunction": forty, thirty, twenty seconds left, so much and no more, a baton is passed, hands touch in vacancy, a glance downward—

Now! The hand grips and pulls—a shocking seizure, flapping aloft, shudder, cessation, gentling, oscillation: a return has been made. The descent under the canopy is related to the dive as youth in its solitary splendid retreat is related to youth in community; it is the act of acceptance that closes the circle, reunites the jumper with nature and conditionedness, re-creates him as one among billions concerned about landing on their feet. Before the act takes place the jumper possesses a heightened reality, understands life as that which a man can take into his own hands and nature as that against which man can act (in certain circumstances) without being crushed; after the act takes place the jumper is part of the given; insofar as the jumper connects the two "phases," he achieves an imitation in little of wholeness or roundedness. But the key to the experience *is* the sharpness of its outline. Once locked in the contained unit or cycle of freedom and conditionedness the chutist knows what cannot be known elsewhere, namely: when, why, and how he must change his relation to otherness, where in freedom the real danger begins. That the diver's panegyric to the dive dwells only on liberty is, in short, deceptive: the prime infatuation, by a paradox, may well be with certitude itself.

The descent from here to allegory requires, as might be guessed, nothing more than a second glance at the chutists' bad gate. Look at us, look at us! the jumpers cried. We imitate life—the pattern of withdrawal and commitment; our leader has quit school to give himself to this task—at twenty-two he has to his credit six hundred and fifty imitations of The Real Thing! But the thin crowd of imperfect adults, caught in roiling Isness, turns away as though replying with the oldest and wannest words: Come down to earth, give over the metaphors and mock-ups: *Live.* Read thus, the allegory is heartening, brighter indeed than can be endured—but shadows can quickly be added. American sky dancers, white, swan-arched, delicately hung in the unbearing air of the binocular lenses, failed to impress their fathers—but they did defeat their opponents: they are the champions, their proficiency is unmatched in the world. Which means? Into that bourne, down or up the cloud ladder, poets only go—but it may as well be noted, for hope's sake, that the first relevant lyrical figure, occurring in a poem titled "On Youth," does (as the epigraph shows) damn descent as escape, and argue that in the wordless clouds no problem is solved.

1962

Dirty Words?

What's fresh? what's hot? what swings with the writing mob? Shhh, baby, not so *loud*. Home and away, among artists and hacks, stillness is In: the move is toward muteness: *silence* is the boffo new literary word.

Every man for himself, of course, in manipulating this Word. In England and West Germany the anti-language line is episte-logico-semantical. The most fashionable English lady novelist of the moment began her career by creating a genius called "The Silencer," a chap who insists that:

Only the greatest men can speak and still be truthful. . . . Only the strongest can rise against [the] weight [of theory]. For most of us, for almost all of us, truth can be attained, if at all, only in silence. [Iris Murdoch, *Under the Net*]

And the coming young German poet, Helmut Heissen-
büttel, asks himself:

—does to distinguish mean to distinguish what from what
    and someone
from someone or simply that it depends and how does one
    distinguish . . . ?

Whereas in France and America you work the vein by
coming on hard against orators. Henri Michaux, who for
years has been cultivating a mystique of the inaudible,
holds that the clearest mark of meanness and stupidity is
adeptness at public speech. (In *Light Through Darkness*
this writer defends hashish on the ground that the hashishee
is a fast man at spotting oratorical sin:

One day when during one of these [hashish] moments I was
looking at a study in a review having a very limited, almost
secret circulation, the study by an erudite young philosopher,
I heard something that sounded like the murmur of crowds
gathered to listen to these words. Well, Well! The sentence,
even when later I read it cold, philosophic though it appeared,
was . . . a sentence that could never come from the pen of
one who had not caressed the idea of appearing . . . on a
platform.)

And J. D. Salinger, zenning against words here at home,
lays it down about the Gettysburg Address that if Lincoln
had been "absolutely honest," he would "simply have come
forward and shaken his fist at his audience" and walked
away without uttering a word.

But while national differences exist, they are not so
pronounced as to threaten the fundamental unity of the
language-baiters—or to inhibit criticism from celebrating

the emergence of a new international literary theme. American partisans of romantic-existential-apocalyptic fiction have, in the course of their celebrations, gone so far as to discover a "tradition" of holy silence-mongering in modern literature. Some among them even declare that language-baiting nowadays reflects "nothing less than the desire to redeem Western values." *

The latter opinion hasn't yet won universal assent, partly because people who back it produce charts of literary "influence," and pairings of literary men, that add up to chaos (Thomas Mann and William Burroughs, for example, or Coleridge and Joseph Heller). Yet this school of critics is by no means insignificant. It has sacred texts— Nietzsche, *Civilization and Its Discontents,* and Norman O. Brown. It offers an uncomplicated version of the genesis and meaning of the attack on public language. (The claim is that the attack can only be understood as a self-less, life-renewing protest against repressive abstraction and order.) And the figures and ideas honored by the school are difficult to dislodge from privileged status. Novelists who pontificate about matters other than the limits of language sooner or later have to face the standard critical queries. How does the story earn the statement? what allowance has been made for experience that contradicts the generalization? But the writer who takes

---

* The phrase occurs in an *American Scholar* essay (Summer 1963) by Ihab Hassan about "the growing distrust of language as a medium of expression, and [the] distrust of form, which has impelled certain modern writers to cultivate chance and disorder. . . ." Hassan discusses a wide range of writers—French Symbolists, Absurd Playwrights, new-wave novelists, Corso-Kerouac, and Salinger himself. Warmly appreciative of the word-baiters, he remarks that "in this strident era of over-communication . . . we are more likely to perish by the word than by the sword, and least of all to perish by a loving silence."

up the theme of silence as glory (or speechmaking as sin) enjoys cosy immunity from the start. Words are the one means of justifying the contention that language is the foe of honesty and reality: how then can you expect a word-hater to explain his hatred?

There are, however, limits to this immunity—or, rather, there ought to be limits to it. No secular literary theme, international or otherwise, benefits from credulous assessment; when literary motives are sanctified or buried beneath fan-letter cant about the "desire to redeem Western values," they become that much more difficult not only for readers but for writers themselves to understand. The need of the moment is for a start toward a historical account of how the word-baiters and silence-mongerers came to be what they are, a survey of the cultural facts underlying bookish assertions that human speech is valueless. Only when this information is in hand will there be much to stop critics turned campaign biographers from transforming authorship into a confidence game.

Where would such an account begin? With politics, social change, and the sociology of writing, of course. Needless to say, a good number of the passionate near-mutes in romantic literature have quasi-religious significance. Symbols like Eliot's "still point"—or Wordsworth's Leechgatherer, or Keats's Urn, or Poe's Raven—illustrate the connection between the imagination of wordlessness and the longing for transcendence. And there are great novelists—Lawrence, Conrad, Tolstoy—whose reflections upon the inadequacies of language stand as footnotes to a large-scale argument against rationalism. (One lesson of *Anna Karenina* is that a man must learn not to define, not to attach words to his feelings, not to state the terms of ideal experience. "What am I about?" Levin asks at the end. "Knowledge, sure, unattainable by reason, has been revealed to me, to my heart, and here am I obstinately trying to express that knowledge in words. . . .")

But while it is clear that the impulse to deprecate language can sometimes be traced to religious hunger for meaning inexpressible in abstractions, it is equally clear that attacks upon the word often have direct social and political reference. Their focus is the lower-class man who has learned to speak up, learned to make himself felt despite the poverty of his birth, education, and training. Flaubert crowded his pages with such men; nowhere in the *Sentimental Education* does his irony carry more contempt than in the descriptions of the citizen-orators of 1848. Zola was interested in the type (in *Germinal* Etienne's virtue is smutched when he shifts from the role of silent witness of suffering to that of the platform agitator). And in the Grand Inquisitor, Dostoevsky brought the character of the wordy usurper to the summit of its development. The Inquisitor's denunciation of Jesus pours on, a furious tide of intellectual passion, for thousands of words; the Listener does not speak. When it is over the Inquisitor sees that:

The Prisoner had been listening intently to him all the time, looking gently into his face and evidently not wishing to say anything in reply. The old man would have liked him to say something, however bitter and terrible. But he suddenly approached the old man and kissed him gently on his bloodless aged lips. That was all his answer.

The writer thus announces that true virtue is wordless. And, through the Inquisitor's speech, he establishes that, in men of power, eloquence is the outward sign of a monstrous inner sin of selfishness.

Why would a writer choose to make this point? In part because of the conviction that, in the post-revolutionary era, eloquence has become a means rather than an end, a gimmick for "improper advancement" rather than a decent symbol of constituted authority (like the mace and robe). The counterpart of this conviction is the belief that in the new world those who manipulate the word are climbing, unentitled, essentially inferior ranters—men who cannot win the authority they covet except by stimulating the lowest self of a mass audience. But it would be a mistake to pretend that either conviction is born of a wholly disinterested, objective contemplation of the run of historical events. Novelists and poets attempt to persuade their audiences to share these convictions not only because the latter are "correct," but because public acceptance of them will advance the literary interest in a vital power struggle.

That the literary interest has been in grave need of advancement for a long while is a commonplace among students of changes in the relation between men of power and men of words. In pre-revolutionary societies of mass illiteracy, possession of the word was a strong guarantee of power. The writer could support his sense of his "difference" not merely by consulting his muse or by pointing at his books, but by reflecting on the quality of his relation to power, and on his position in the social hierarchy. The difference was, in fact, less immediately psychological than socio-economic. Only the elite manipulated symbols: governors and wordmen were, in relative terms, at one.

But the word belonged to everyman after the flood, as already observed. (A half-hour session of Flaubert's "Club of Intellect" includes orations from adolescents, printers, lunatic professors, farmer-priests, shopmen, wine salesmen, and masons—not to mention passing drunks and bums.) And, harassed by the "competition" of people who only a generation before hadn't dared even to think, much less to talk or write, writers intent upon maintaining a place were badly placed. One alternative was to search out, from among a muddle of possible constituencies, some comparatively inarticulate group that might still be considered "in need of a voice." The other was to offer a representation of the world of universal talk that established *silence,* the eschewal of words, as the defining characteristic of the natural aristocrat.

More than one major novelist of the century refused to be trapped into an irrevocable choice between these options. Dickens speaks for a group he imagines to be inarticulate ("Dead, your Majesty. Dead, my lords and gentlemen . . ."), as though resigned to a position away from the center of power. But many of his symbols and comic inventions express longing for the obliteration of the racketing voices which, in the new civilization, diffuse the power of the word. Conrad takes as a theme the emptiness of the rhetoric of "Christian imperialism," but simultaneously makes himself a spokesman for an undiscovered, uncounted constituency: the exploited pagan horde.

In the long sweep of post-revolutionary time, however,

it grew increasingly difficult even for the most gifted and self-assured artist to keep his poise in the face of endlessly multiplying scribblers and oratorical fantasts. And the well-known result was that writers in great numbers gave up the search for constituencies, and rejected the notion that the attention of a man of power was worth striving for.

That this choice did not mean a total loss of audience isn't mysterious. Post-revolutionary events both intellectual and social helped to create a climate favorable to mockery of the pretensions of magistrates and governors. Late-nineteenth-century ideas of culture, class, and consciousness weakened faith in governors as men of another order of being. (*All* men are bound by myth, repression, and economic interest.) And the governors themselves spent little effort in maintaining the social forms which, even after a revolution, might have lent special authority to their words. Their slobbish behavior practically enforced upon all ascendant democrats a view of balanced sentences and elevated speech as dress-up. And the prevalence of this view in turn guaranteed that the displaced writer who leered at speechmakers (he'll be loosening that collar later on, why not now?) would run no risk of offending his audience.

But to be in contact with such an audience—climbers, outsiders, and other ordinary folk who read with their lips —was small satisfaction for literary men. So long as a novelist merely teased managerial or legislative chatterers and rhetoricians, after the fashion of Mark Twain, he functioned as the voice of the democratic wave that had swamped him; by hinting that leaders were just folks, he reassured citizens that no word and no power could be higher than theirs. To clear a way toward a place of distinction comparable to the one he had lost, the writer needed first of all to dissociate himself completely from barroom-barbershop opinionators, Rotary ranters, and letters-to-the-editor men on the one hand, and from the ghostwritten culture of the false elite on the other. He could take a step toward this end by adopting tones of detached generalizing contempt, and by dramatizing the powerlessness of the new officeholders. (The dominant theme of the nineteenth-century political novel is that of the unmanageability of events, military, diplomatic, economic.) But the direct course was to find means of effecting a redistribution of the property—language itself— whose reality as power was most palpable to him as literary man.

Just here lay the usefulness of the theme of silence, and of the new polarity of abstraction versus existence. The invention of a super- or anti- language about language (one that devalued the mass-owned word) could not be expected to refurbish the old alliance of governors and littérateurs, or to reopen old lines of communication. The terms of the super-language were magical, exempt from the "limits of words," incapable of being blended into debate in the great chamber of "lies" inhabited by managers of public affairs. But the new language could bring about the collapse of distinctions between the false elite and the masses; it enabled the writer to stand before his audience as a priest before a congregation of identical human beings, all of whom were inferior to him by virtue of the inadequacies of their language and their unawareness thereof. And this was, for literary men, an essential turn of events. As long as the high public estimate of the value of public words ("free speech") went uncontested, he couldn't raise his voice, hence could not rise. But when that estimate was cast in doubt, a dozen possibilities emerged. In the act of calling for an end to abstraction he could set taboos on the language of the mighty as well as of the base. By directing his fury at the sin of "hypostatization" he could shame the world for having failed to give him its word. And by creating silence as the only conceivable redeemer for non-literary man, he might well restore the uniqueness stripped from him by egalitarians at the hour of the socialization of the word.

Every reader will think of his own examples of work touched by these motives and themes. Eliot's *Coriolan,* read as a political rather than religious poem, is a perfect paradigm of the politics of silence: a voiceless true leader is set in absolute opposition to a quacking vox populi. Powerless orators and masscult monologuists are prime objects of mockery in Joyce's *Ulysses:* one function of myth in this book is to dramatize differences between the world as it was when the elite owned the word and as it is when every shopgirl has a "literary imagination" (Nausicaa against Gerty McDowell). And the shape of Joyce's career betrays a determination to exact public acknowledgment that his language is remote from that of governors and proles. But the most telling evidence of the reality of the themes in question is that serious books have actually taken as their subject the writer's need for a unique "line" about language that will deliver him from impotence.

Consider for example the novel of Iris Murdoch's that was quoted earlier. The chief figures of *Under the Net* are, by name, Jake Donaghue and Hugo Belfounder; the relation between them is described by the narrator as "the central theme of [the] book." At the opening of the tale Donaghue is a talented but feckless mooching hack and translator, penniless, homeless, unlucky in love; Belfounder, on the other hand, is a powerful manager, blessed with a "unique intellectual and moral quality," lucky in love, and wealthy (he has made successive fortunes in the armament and motion-picture industries, because he inspires "universal confidence" and has "an iron nerve"). Jake Donaghue's friends attribute his failure to develop his literary gifts to laziness, but, as the course of the story makes clear, that explanation is too easy. The fact is that early in his writing life Jake became acquainted with Belfounder, and was dazzled by what seemed an overwhelmingly original and persuasive set of ideas about language. Belfounder's ideas are the staple stuff of the language-baiter: words are but a veil, "all stories [are] lies," "*actions* [alone] don't lie," "truth can be attained . . . only in silence." But they have a paralyzing effect upon Jake Donaghue. He cannot discount them as products of writerly bitterness about mass-age men of action who cynically cut themselves in on the power of the word. Belfounder isn't a writer but a man of action: he not only possesses power *and* the word but even, as it appears, the girl Jake loves: he inspires terror, not analysis. Jake does, in the early sequel, flee in fear from Belfounder; he avoids appointments with him, eventually changes his domicile in order to escape the man's eye. But the flight that counts, as

an expression of terror, is the retreat from a career: Jake
disowns his ambition and lapses into relative silence.

Viewed as a dramatization of deficiencies of modern
literary power, this novelistic situation presents no severe
problems of interpretation. Miss Murdoch's story is about
the theft of the muse by the manager—a flat reversal, as
it were, of Camus's dictum that "we must make . . . our
poets into captains of industry"; its one bold trick is the
identification of the muse with the theme of silence itself.
The latter theme is, to repeat, both shield and weapon for
the post-revolutionary writer; by deprecating the word he
(in fantasy) seizes a place above the word-owning masses,
and above the false elite (managers, men of action) as
well. And therefore the expropriation of the theme by a
manager is a double frustration for a writer—an event
out of which much dramatic capital can be made. The
capital is not wasted in *Under the Net*. Time and again
the novelist brings into sight a character or event eligible
for the irony of a word-baiter (mass-age political oratory
is ridiculed in a chaotic scene presenting a labor-union
leader incompetently addressing a crowd of workers on a
movie set—from a prop Roman chariot). And time and
again Jake Donaghue the writer witnesses the event, or
observes the character, in the company of the word-baiting
man of power—and suffers accordingly, since such occasions deprive him even of an illusion that his responses
are unique.

But *Under the Net* is about recovery as well as about
theft. Absorbed at the start with Donaghue's frustrations,
the book subsequently recounts his progress toward a
renewal of faith. And, as might be expected, the moment of

crisis in the progress occurs when Jake recovers silence
as a theme of his own creation.

The novelist works with some ingenuity to prepare for
this moment. She assigns the position of narrator to her
hero, the writer, thereby freeing herself from the obligation
to explain fully his mistakes of perception. The scenes in
which the man of power seems, to Jake's mind, to be
developing his subtle views about the limits of language
are done largely in indirect discourse. These views are at
length made known to the reader through excerpts from
a book of dialogues called *The Silencer* that Jake himself
has composed, in theory as a representation of Belfounder's
thinking. By a careful manipulation of events the revelation of Belfounder's reaction to this document is postponed
to the end of the tale. And before that moment occurs
the reader has been offered several hints that Jake Donaghue is a self-deceived character who perversely attributes
to the man of action ideas that are in fact his own.

But despite the elaborate preparations, the turnabout
encounter between writer and manager in which the manager insists that the ideas about language in *The Silencer*
actually belong to the writer, not to him, is awkward and
unconvincing. The once self-sufficient man of power becomes, too suddenly, a figure ridden with envy of the
literary artist. ("Wherever did you get all those ideas from?
. . . Your thing [*The Silencer*] was so clear. I learnt an
awful lot from it.") The explanation of Jake's original awe
is lame. (" 'The trouble with you, Jake,' said [Belfounder],
'is that you're far too impressed by people. You were far
too impressed by me. . . . You can . . . create things.
. . . I never made a thing in my life.' ") And the reversal

of positions—Belfounder humiliated, the writer elevated —is melodramatic in execution. (The manager gives up his power and goes off to a job in the provinces as a watchmaker, and the writer returns to *The Silencer* and his other manuscripts, aware at last that the themes expressed in these works are not only his own but, potentially, the substance of significant works of art.)

The likelihood is that the author of *Under the Net* was clear neither about her ideas nor about the best means of embodying them in believable sequences of human action. The ambiguity of the arguments "for and against language" is one visible sign of unease; Miss Murdoch is far more comfortable when dealing with linguistic issues as part of intellectual history (see her criticism), than when confronting them as determinants of human behavior. Other signs are the contrived quality of the denouement, and the frenzied injection of brawls and high jinks (the book is filled with what became, in the Angry novelists, the standard junk of mid-twentieth-century picaresque). But the question of the quality of the book is for the moment irrelevant. What matters is that *Under the Net* is, demonstrably, a narrative based on the assumption that possessiveness about the word and resentment of the expropriation of language by non-writers are genuine facts of feeling for the modern writer. And the action of the work is ruled from beginning to end by a conception of the theme of silence as both strategy and therapy—the one means by which writers can effect the emasculation of their oppressors and the restoration of their own potency.

The same uses of the theme are visible in the fiction of J. D. Salinger. The case of Seymour Glass is, to be sure, superficially dissimilar to that of Jake Donaghue. Seymour's creator presents himself as a man concerned not primarily about writers but about the common fate of sensitive men. And as a consequence his manner of articulating the theme of literary power-through-silence is more oblique than Iris Murdoch's. Yet, as everyone knows, Salinger is not in the habit of keeping distance between himself and his sensitive protagonists; their agonies become his, the torments of a writer caged in the modern world. And his stories insist that the least tolerable of these agonies is the endless, meaningless, hopelessly barren yammering of the figures who conceive themselves to be the practical managers of this world.

Few things are plainer in Salinger's fiction than his desire that his complaint against non-literary or pseudo-literary wordmongers be understood as a religious gesture, a protest against selfishness and for organic existence. The Glass family stories are decorated with a score of epigraphs, excerpts from fables, and aphorisms whose burden is the incommensurateness of language to life; Seymour himself insists that "the human voice conspires to desecrate every thing on earth." And enthusiasts of Salinger have made much of these decorations, even arguing that the work they adorn develops a "sacramental notion of silence." But while there is no denying the intensity of the writer's feeling for silence as a value, neither is there reason to doubt that this value, as expressed in a Salinger story, is a strategy as well as a sacrament. The world of these stories is composed of two camps: people of apparent power, people of apparent powerlessness. The villainous wordmongers—brisk, manipulative, self-confident, exactly rendered managers—are characters of apparent power. The sensitive word-baiting protagonists—writers all in essence (whether by profession or in embryo)—are people of apparent powerlessness, helpless types whom the yakking managers ceaselessly harry into and out of classrooms, rest rooms, hotels, bathtubs, marriages, careers. . . . And it is in the context of this seeming imbalance of power that both the human and political dimensions of Salinger's protest against the word appear. The aim of the protest isn't only to lay on the record an impersonal plea for non-abstract existence; it is also to recover magical potencies for literary man—by devaluing the chatter of the Lane Coutells of the world, figures of phony authority and competence.

Nor is the protest limited to canting undergraduates or dirty-word scribblers or efficient Moms—witness the ruminations about Lincoln and Gettysburg mentioned above. These diary entries of Seymour's have bearings at once broader and subtler than those of the ordinary paradox of purity (we are all murderers, none of us is innocent enough to speak). When Seymour envisions absolute honesty at Gettysburg as incapable of more than a fist-shaking gesture, one of his effects is to characterize the honest *political* leader as a man unutterably remote, separated both from the people he leads and from the events that occur during his tenure. For Salinger's audience the fruit of this invention is a release. To understand the Presidency as powerless whenever decent is to banish the idea of responsibility and wash everyman's hand of the Whole Thing. If authority cannot be virtuous, or if virtue become a head of state can only turn on the nation and chide it for its actions, then chaos and corruption are natural laws, and no individual citizen needs to concern himself with the national events that occur in his lifetime. But for the writer there is a release of a different order—release from the wearing pressure of belief that the chatterers, the figures of apparent strength (whether "great orators" or bathroom barkers), in truth possess any power whatever. I, the mute but revealed Honest Seymour-Abe, started nothing, managed nothing, finished nothing: things happened "out there," stupidity in the mass drove them on, authority was never more than helpless, there are no men at the top. The writer asserts through his hero that if he as writer cannot be competent and responsible, if he as writer cannot be a man of power, then power does not exist: the word-mongering false elite should admit its futility and subside.

Inherent in this logic is an ideal of political virtue impossible enough, perhaps, to be described as religious. But examination of the conflicts elsewhere in Salinger's fiction indicates that the writer's vision of honesty stems only in part from torment about the gap between reality and the ideal. Its ultimate spring may well be *ressentiment* itself, a motive of revenge—a will to strike back at the non-writers of the immediate circle, and through them at doltish pseudo-leaderly millions of others who, sure of their own tongue, have dismissed the literary imagination as a superfluity.

Parallels to the situations and conflicts just discussed can be located in a great number of contemporary writers —but a multiplication of instances would be evasive. And the same can be said of efforts to decide whether word-baiting is one more special "sickness" of the age.* The plain case is that not for a century or more has adoption of a "healthy" attitude toward language been a living alternative for literary man. The modern writer who damns the word, the modern technician or scientist who trusts it "within limits," are both conditioned by general history and by the history of literacy itself. For the technician, a man without precedents who understands that he has everything to gain, the response cannot be unfavorable. For the writer, a man whose gift can never again be an indisputable mark of command, the response cannot be favorable. The latter isn't alone in his sense of loss; other men of mind in his age are engaged in efforts to recover mastery of language as the defining property of the elite. It is by no means fanciful to hold that most of the new academic enterprises of the humanities in this century—analytical philosophy, linguistics, semantics, the new techniques of literary criticism, the very emergence of literature as a study—owe their inception in part to the desire of the clerk to repossess himself of mystery, to take language out of the public domain, to give just deserts to an

---

* For the record it may as well be noted, though, that freedom from voices that talk judgmentally back out of the air is a deep longing of the paranoiac; the latter uses his own speech as a means of silencing other speakers whose words threaten his being. In the chapters on the madness of D. P. Schreber which conclude his *Crowds and Power*, Elias Canetti has a valuable commentary on the subject. Culling evidence from the memoirs of Schreber, who was Senatspräsident of the Dresden Court of Appeals until his illness, Canetti observes that "the thing most important to [this madman] was the safety of words. To him all sounds were voices, the universe was full of words: railways, birds and paddle-steamers spoke. When he was not uttering words himself they immediately came from others. *Between* words there was nothing. The peace he spoke of and longed for would have been a *freedom from words*. But this was not to be found."

age in which everyman believes he owns and understands the word. But solidarity with these inquirers promises nothing to the writer: they too are competitors, violators of literary power. Far from offering him a restorative community, they deepen his depression, sharpen his conviction that silence must be his theme.

It is one thing, however, to grant the inevitability of this theme, the total absence of alternatives (healthy, convalescent, or whatever), and another to stand abashed in its presence. The reader who dismisses the theme of silence as a rare paranoiac infection misreads the past: in the twentieth century there is no way for the writer to meet his need for self-trust save by deprecating the word of others. The reader who argues that the attack upon the word is propelled only by a sensible desire to dramatize scientific discoveries—as, for example, that language is no mirror, and the thingy world is a dream—scores a debater's point (while oversimplifying the relation between art and the history of ideas). But the reader who claims that a novelistic sermon on the inadequacies of language, or a passage of abuse of the Gettysburg Address, or an advertisement of a writer's availability as a candidate for the Presidency, is in its pure and single essence a reaction to repressive modern civilization is a sentimentalist. Because he refuses to allow for the effect of feelings of powerlessness upon any man's attitude toward power, this reader confuse acts of self-interest with acts of self-renunciation.

And there is, to repeat, only one way out of the confusion. The new clichés must earn their keep or lose it in face-to-face encounter with the contention that their roots lie in narrowly private interest. To confront them in the

stance of the ready-made convert is to turn mindlessness itself into a value.

The significance of this conclusion can of course be
enlarged. For there is at least a possibility that the fury
directed at other appurtenances of post-revolutionary civilization besides language may also be subject to analysis
as a mode of revenge. Critics who deny this possibility,
stoutly maintaining that the ideal reader of modern literature can only be a convert, run no risk of the charge of
inhumanity; they prove their openness to literary assault
by rising bewildered and disturbed from apocalyptic texts.
(The example of Professor Trilling comes to mind.) And
the same cannot always be said of those who are eager to
shrug off literary damnation of the age: their common
conclusion, namely that at the present moment every
educated citizen is wiser as well as stupider than the wisest
writer, because freer of the past, is too often proclaimed as
a triumph.

But rivalries for the crown of Sensibility shouldn't be
allowed to obscure the truth that the lesson implicit in
the writings of word-baiters does have substantial weight
of its own. Accepting the silent saint as a wholly disinterested, self-renouncing redeemer not only means being
oblivious to a subtle power grab, a sly act of aggression.
It also requires a pretense that alienation never deflects,
never embitters, never blinds, the mind that suffers it. And
this pretense, whether cruel or generous to those who
believe with Seymour-Abe that no one but the writer "*has*
to speak," does severe damage to the largest human causes
that literature is presumed to serve. "If one starts de-

ploring the inadequacy of language to reality," Sartre once
remarked, "one makes oneself an accomplice of the enemy,
that is, of propaganda." The struggle to hold free of such
complicity is, as the remark implies, a struggle for the
survival of means of compelling rulers as well as rhymers
to give their open word. Everywhere the century testifies
that this struggle is neither abstract nor "existentially"
corrupt. Everywhere the century testifies that in its defeat
casualties heavier by millions than at Gettysburg go down,
poets and proles inseparable in the mass.

1965

Party Apolitics

Tradition ruled the preliminaries. Letters to delegates teemed with clichés ("If you think of me now and remember me," wrote a State Senator declaring for the Attorney Generalship, "I promise you I will do no less for you in the future"), as did the monthly flyers ("PEABODY PROGRAM LABELLED PARTNERSHIP FOR PROGRESS"), the billboard admonitions "Judge-Analyze-Compare-Test!! . . . Senator Caples Qualifies!!"), and even the telegraphed pledges of eats ("CORDIALLY INVITE YOU TO HAVE DINNER WITH ME . . . HAVE MANY IMPORTANT STATE PROBLEMS TO DISCUSS WITH YOU, HOPE YOU CAN ATTEND. WARM REGARDS. LIEUT. GOVERNOR EDWARD F. MCLAUGHLIN JR."). The rather grand hired hall, Springfield's Memorial Auditorium, was beflagged and bepostered into the repetitious squalor ever regarded as appropriate for

party assemblage. And inside it the apparatus of Big-time
Politics (heat, sweat, bad cigars, pages, parliamentarians,
sergeants at arms, tally clerks, TV crews, Committeemen,
cops, gossip, gavels, and hard-sell plastic fans) was nothing if not conventional. But although conclaves of citizens
had met before and would meet again on similar business
(that of choosing slates of candidates for state and federal
offices), few had faced situations comparable to those confronting the Democratic conclave at hand. And for that
reason stubbornness persisted in claiming that the occasion
couldn't possibly be routine.

By far the most striking of the situations mentioned was,
of course, the chief contest itself, which pitted a brother
of the President against a nephew of the Speaker of the
United States House of Representatives. But there were
others of equal if less publicized note. For one: Democrats
were troubled by unusually insistent intimations of disaster
at the polls. (In 1960 the party's gubernatorial candidate
was badly defeated; scandals in the intervening period had
induced fresh feelings of unease; and, as a consequence,
tolerance of hell-raising, hair-pulling, and schemes to
solve economic problems by means of a state sweepstakes
—items that had figured in the party's Boston Arena
gathering two years before—was plainly on the decline.)
For another: word was out that the nation's interest in
the convention was to be focused largely through the eyes
of first-string Washington correspondents, men habituated
to political dispute slightly more elegant than the Bay
State's, and therefore likely to function unconsciously—
perhaps merely by asking clear questions—as influential
forces for good. (The expectation about press attendance

proved correct: among the hundreds of reporters were many whose typewriter cases bore tags marked "Trip of the President," and there were in addition—so said rumor —a number of highly placed Specials on the scene: a liberal Saltonstall telling all for the *New Republic,* a relative of the late J. P. Marquand making of the occasion something fit for *Show.*) And for still another: the affair was to mark the first public encounter between old-line party regulars and a band of reformers calling itself the Commonwealth Organization of Democrats—a group that was pursuing a vigorous campaign to "overhaul the Democratic Party in Massachusetts."

Observers who saw in the prospect of this encounter possibilities for a significant turn in the direction of Bay State politics were responding in part to the energy and militancy of the leaders of the Commonwealth Organization (COD). The latter had fought hard for open discussion of the urgent organizational problems of their party. They had announced their intention of "financing and sponsoring twenty to thirty COD candidates for the State Legislature in 1962," and of running their own candidates "for every seat on the Democratic State Committee" two years hence. They had also laid down a demand that a serious, strong-minded party platform be shaped and debated before and during the convention, and, with the intention of avoiding the "chaos and confusion" of earlier parleys, they had gone so far as to send six single-spaced pages of recommendations on the conduct of the convention to the Chairman of the State Committee. The recommendations were solemn (COD was even stern about music: "All bands and formal parades will be eliminated.

. . . The hall, of course, should be equipped with an organ for the playing of the National Anthem. No other musical instrument appears necessary or desirable"). And they met no warm welcome (a State Committee spokesman apparently well-disposed to song told a reporter that, so far as conventions were concerned, the State Committee's job was simply that of "dropping a nickel into the slot and letting it [the convention] play its own music"). But the remark was defensive, and the reformers' hopes survived it. Their claim, tirelessly repeated, was that because the party offers "little more than intra-party feuds, rival organizations built around individual office-holders, ineptness at the State House, and public scandals," it was under a special obligation to define its internal problems and commit itself to solutions. And few voices were raised in public criticism of their goals.

That the goals were not achieved at the convention means neither that old-style "chaos and confusion" was everywhere the rule, nor that the occasion was, as press cynics predicted, merely routine. For the press indeed, there was at all moments matter of high interest. There were glimpses of a few of the great sights of Massachusetts' political life: John F. Thompson (called the "Iron Duke" or "The Tyrant of Ludlow"), a power in the Massachusetts House currently praised and dispraised for the style in which, as Speaker, he gavels down the opposition ("At various times I have let things in for all of you. You don't want me to get real rough and start blocking things, do you?"); Bernard Cleary, the smiling, huge-girthed, black-suited Mayor of Taunton known as "The Happy Undertaker" to the faithful who support his biannual, un-

successful bids for one or another state office; the trio of
famous nicknames—Mucker McGrath, Sonny McDon-
ough, Knocko McCormack (the latter, father of Mr. Ed,
the state's Attorney General, is a cool beefy leader popular in part for his habit of maintaining poise by shedding
clothing). There were girls, girls, girls—parades (without
music) of white-clad maidens with baskets of posies (enthusiasts of Mr. Kevin White, Secretary of State), and
blue-clad maidens in red sailor hats (enthusiasts of Mr.
Ted Kennedy). There was an official committee meeting
—on disputed slates of delegates—that issued in a call
for police. (Before and after their arrival, as the creden-
tials group rejected a number of delegates presumed to be
pledged to Mr. McCormack, several occurrences reddened
the face of Reform: walkouts by committee members who
charged indecorously that "This is the most rigged god-
dam thing in the world," arguments marked by cries of
"Communist!" and "Throw the bum out!," overhomely
"explanations" of decisions by old accrediting hands like
Mr. Bill Boyle, who at one point informed a contesting
delegate that State Committee secretaries "got no more
right to tell you to make a slate [of delegates] than the
bartender downstairs.")

Beyond these incidental amusements, there were two
press conferences that rank among the most and least
successful ventures of their kind undertaken by candidates
for major public office in recent years. Faced with harsh
queries from out-of-state reporters, Mr. Ted Kennedy,
who a few hours later, atop a sound truck amid a madly
cheering mob, delivered a lashing, raucous belt of a fight
talk in the manner of late Willie Stark or early Honey

Fitz, responded with a shy amiable gentleness that was almost wholly winning. Faced with friendly questions, the
latter's opponent, Mr. McCormack, an able pipe-smoking
young lawyer with a boyish wave, narrow face, tight ears,
and an unfortunate slouch to his lower lip, simply could
not find a likable tone. (He accused the Kennedy camp of
exerting unfair pressure on delegates, and refused to produce his evidence on the ground that to do so would be to
hurt the President; he argued that in running against the
President's brother he was "doing the President a favor,"
saving him from "the dynasty issue"; and always as he
spoke, smiling brightly, his eyes had a curious inwardness,
watchful, uncertain—the disquieting gaze of the man
whose half-conscious awareness that he is failing seems
about to drive him into some unimaginable extravagance.)
And there were endless side bars of color—a retired
prize-fighter, Rocky Marciano of Brockton, appearing
loyally in support of a schoolboy chum turned political
aspirant; a full-blooded Indian from Gay Head in horned
headdress, who allowed that "I'm taking the next bus out
of here unless I can convince them to my way of thinking"; and more than a few troubling ironies. (In front of
the auditorium marched two supporters of H. Stuart
Hughes who were advertising the petition drive to secure
for their man a place on the ballot as an Independent
candidate responsive to SANE; they wore sandwich posters that read, SAVE OUR CHILDREN, and touched shoulders
with McCormack supporters whose posters claimed: BET-
TER ED THAN TED.) And at length there were the formal
endorsements of Mr. Kennedy and of—a number of

others whose names the out-of-state pressmen did not tarry to learn.

But while all this did offer a measure of entertainment, it remained (to repeat) less than what the reformers had hoped for. And however unrealistic the expectations, the ensuing disappointment was not easy to shrug away. It was clear that a meeting at which a bitter intraparty struggle is waged between two strong "personal factions" is not propitious for consideration of specific steps toward organizational reform. (The changes mentioned included the provision of "coordinating and communicating devices" between local town committees and the State Committee, new methods of dispensing patronage without secrecy, extensions of the governor's authority as party leader, and shifts in fund-raising procedures that would restore the responsibility for this activity to local Democratic committees—"with money raised at that level being funneled upward to the state committee rather than the other way around.") And it was equally clear that, although highly significant causal relations exist between lax party discipline and corruption in government—the latter continues to be a major issue here in Massachusetts —firm discipline would not solve every problem. (Corruption thrives in the "Commonwealth" partly because of the nature of the state government itself, which assigns the management of a number of important public affairs to autonomous units—among them a covey of authorities for land-taking, parks, and turnpikes—with questionable methods of requisitioning and contracting.)

But concern at the evidence that the still small voice

of COD was still small was traceable not only to premonitions of continuing scandals. The case was that, after the Republican opposition had held its conclave, and the lines of pre-primary strategy for both parties had come clear, the evasion of party problems stood forth in a new context—as fresh evidence of a general political trend that rouses not disappointment but fear.

The trend in question—toward an apolitical politics, partyless and problemless—can be assessed in accordance with a dozen commonplaces of political knowledge. It is not news, surely, that most citizens are disinclined to task their minds with complex subjects. (In his *Economic Theory of Democracy,* Anthony Downs offered a model of the voter as consumer, and noted that acceptance of political clichés can be regarded as an act of thrift, since the serious investigation of issues and qualifications requires expenditures of time and money; this account of the ordinary citizen also holds for delegates to party conventions.) And it is equally well known that great numbers of citizens consider the public issues of desperate current urgency to be remote from state affairs. (Sympathy for this view inspired Professor Hughes's petitionary efforts, and discouraged John F. Kennedy as Senator from taking an active role in reorganizing state party affairs; it also encouraged Mr. Kennedy as President to defend his brother's candidacy for the Senate with the remark that, after all, "public life is centered, in at least the great issues, in the United States Capitol.") In many minds here and elsewhere the conviction grows that, owing to the ever-broadening influence of the national government and to the increasingly firm grip of mass (nationally uniform) culture on the public mind, the state is in some sense obsolete.

But despite all this, the behavior and gestures of the candidates themselves at the conventions, and the assumptions voiced in conversation by the delegates, couldn't be fully understood in the familiar terms of voter apathy or obsolescent states. Not the least notable feature of this behavior was the extraordinary *consciousness* among participants in the gatherings of popular disaffection with politics. A common remark at both conventions was that the best qualification for any aspirant for state office was, if not lack of experience, then lack of identification in the public mind with ward politics, office-holding, loyal party labor, or the power of insiderdom. And the viewpoint was not difficult to support. The Democratic Convention endorsed the President's brother, newer to Massachusetts politics than his opponent, and a number of other candidates who had held no major state office. And the Republican Convention, which two years ago had won with a "new face" in the gubernatorial race, gave its Senatorial endorsement to Mr. George Lodge, who in turn was far fresher to state politics than his opponent, Representative Lawrence Curtis (a longtime member of the Massachusetts Congressional delegation). But these decisions were at best minor parts of the tale. What counted far more in stimulating the notion that unfamiliar political elements were at work was the grand strategy favored by the candidates seeking endorsement. Every candidate appeared to be engaged in an attempt first to establish himself as a political innocent, second to link the opposition with professional politics and insiderdom.

Some of the gestures favored by the grand strategists were, to be sure, of less than overwhelming interest. The decision of Mr. Endicott Peabody, who was endorsed by the Democrats for the Governorship, to forgo an ordinary campaigning tour in favor of a "family camping tour through Massachusetts"—Mr. Peabody caught poison ivy shortly after this trip began—earns a place only in the annals of political jokes. (As a Boston Yankee, a public-spirited lawyer with a private practice, and an intelligent supporter of COD, Mr. Peabody had ample qualifications as a maverick on the Democratic ticket before he set out on his trip.) But the terms of the Kennedy-McCormack contest were striking. As indicated, these candidates did not possess the same amount of political experience—but neither was a stranger to the world of politics. Mr. McCormack had held a succession of elective offices since 1953; Mr. Kennedy had had a family acquaintance with politics since boyhood, and had played a major role in his brother's campaign for the Presidency; both men bore renowned political names. It seemed impossible that either could hope to present himself as an amateur. But in the sequel both men embraced the new style: each presented himself as a political outsider, each sought to tar his opponent as an insider.

Mr. McCormack's efforts in this line were the more tortured, because of his temptation to praise his own public service even as he presented himself as a political innocent. The thrust of his attack went to the charge that

Mr. Kennedy *was* Politics itself—politics as promises, threats, postmasterships, federal jobs, deals, men of power lighting each other's candles. Before the convention made its choice, Mr. McCormack spoke to the delegates in the voice of one who understood that they were Little People tired of being mauled and manipulated by Big Men in Big Jobs; he would give them the kind of "recognition" that only an outsider feels obliged to give to another outsider. After the toss had gone against him, he turned from the delegates to registered Democrats generally, and appealed to *their* sense of themselves as the true victims of political chicanery. Conventions, he maintained, are meaningless, since "most [delegates] are depending upon politics for a living"—that is, are of the strictly political Establishment that repudiated him. Describing his opponent's victory as a "demonstration of raw political power . . . and resources," he himself declared his interest in and need for one-dollar and five-dollar contributions: gifts of the humble to the humble. And as the campaign progressed he made less and less of his connection with official party affairs (the connection had been close at one point: a hundred-dollar-a-plate dinner had raised more than a hundred thousand dollars for the McCormack campaign not long before the convention).

Since Mr. Kennedy was known to be a very young man, his task of creating himself as an innocent was simpler than Mr. McCormack's—but there was room for some subtlety. This candidate refused every invitation to refute the charge that he lacked experience; he avoided state issues in his speeches; and, with an air implying that local technicalities are fascinating only to men immersed in power, he talked Washington and Victory to the virtual exclusion of other subjects. There were moments during the pre-convention campaign when the easy confidence of his portrayal of a nervous non-politician owed much to the (unintended) coaching of the McCormack forces, who for a time seemed determined to press charges of youth and irresponsibility against him. (Before the need to dissociate himself from authority became evident, Mr. McCormack referred constantly to his opponent as "Teddie," thereby condescending from the heights of age, which are easily confused with the summits of power; in addition he accused Mr. Kennedy of failing to vote in elections in which he was eligible to vote, as though unaware that this failure itself might strike others, paradoxically, as a guarantee of exalted disinterest.) But on many occasions Mr. Kennedy acted brilliantly for himself. At candidates' forums his was invariably the outside chair, and while he was in it he engaged in no friendly banter with the others on the podium, took scrupulous notes on the remarks of those who spoke before him, and only infrequently smiled. He often sent out mail on plain white sheets that bore nothing at the top except his name. (Other non-office-holding candidates who lacked official note paper used blaring colored heads that announced the addresses and telephones of their campaign headquarters.) When appearing in public he walked alone, eschewing the company of the multiple aides, protectors, and advisers usually found at candidates' ears and elbows. And in a dozen other ways he helped to shape himself into the type of the earnest unknown, the man accustomed to being forgotten by the Organization.

For reasons already cited, an especial significance attaches to the attempts of Democratic candidates to show themselves as green hands at the organization of party power. But this hardly means that the similar attempts visible at Worcester, scene of the Republican Convention in mid-June, were without importance. In a sense the attempts are traditional at conclaves of Bay State Republicans. Measured by voter registrations both the Democrats and the Republicans are "minority parties" in Massachusetts, where a million residents are registered as Independents; but Democrats have a three-to-two edge in party registrations, and therefore the state G.O.P. rarely trumpets the party affiliations of its major candidates. (Governor Volpe's successful campaign in 1960 was made on the slogan "Vote the Man, Vote Volpe," which appeared on billboards bare of reference to the Republican Party.) Still, the impression was that Republican preconvention campaign style this year aimed at a closer approach to apolitics than had been attempted in the past. Representative Lawrence Curtis, seeking the Senatorial endorsement, employed a strategy that directly paralleled Mr. McCormack's; he turned attention away from his long experience in Congress, and developed astonishing strength as a wise country amateur seeking to try his rude underprivileged hand ("I have no famous relatives") in the great world after a decade in the Congressional barn. And, more important, the convention as a whole repeatedly showed its impatience with "narrow party talk."

As should be said, this behavior can be regarded as a careless indulgence of the kind permitted only to strength. For historical reasons—among them the simplicity of its "ethnic make-up"—the Republican Party is more or less untroubled by organizational chaos. But the eruptions of non-commitment at Worcester seemed part of a pattern of embarrassment at political labels inexplicable in purely historical terms. Mr. Lodge strengthened his position at a critical point by releasing a private poll that showed him running much stronger than Representative Curtis among Independent voters (in races against Democratic candidates described only as "A" and "B"). Some Republicans were irritated by this news, naturally: as young Mr. Lodge pressed through the crowd to the rostrum to accept the congratulations of Senator Saltonstall, a voice rang around the hall at a captured microphone, droning for all to hear: "George Lodge is a Democrat! George Lodge is a Democrat!" But that error of taste went unchided. And when, a few moments later at a press conference, a reporter asked Mr. Lodge whether he was a "liberal Republican," the assembled observers—including the Governor, who had run as a Man—witnessed another graceful glide away from parties "and all that." Mr. Lodge met the question in what might well have been called the characteristic convention style of 1962, one that deprecates every label that brings to mind organized politics, announces boredom with leftists, rightists, liberals, conservatives, Republicans, Democrats, and manages to locate the issues off the page, beyond words, beyond quarrel. "I am not a—" the candidate began, and then broke off, adding after a moment, with a pleasant smile: "I deny the word, I have denied the *words,* they are meaningless."

What significance is to be attached to such denials? No doubt it is overfanciful to claim that the candidates who

make them are groping for candidacies beyond politics—
but it is a fact that large audiences for candidacies of this
kind already exist. Public disapproval of "party business"
crops out in the least as well as in the most sophisticated
attempts to register the popular pulse. (An inquiring photographer of the Boston *Herald* asking a question in June
about the value of political conventions drew a number
of relevant answers: "The voters have no say at all. . . ."
". . . the pressure groups are going to rule anyway."
"There's where the political machines operate.") The
figure of the political outsider—Mr. George Romney is
the latest recruit to the legion—has grown steadily more
familiar. Political talent scouts like Representative Bob
Wilson of California, Chairman of the Republican Congressional Committee, are said to be advising local party
leaders to worry more about vivacity and less about party
regularity or ideology in choosing young candidates. And
public scorn for party men (together with disbelief in issues) is now regarded by academic political scientists as
an element of sufficient importance to justify serious efforts to frame a descriptive politics of alienation.

The most successful effort in the field thus far is that of
Professor Murray B. Levin of Boston University. Professor Levin finds outmoded the old theory of the "ethnically
balanced ticket"; arguing that the sound politician does
well to "plan his campaign by dividing the electorate into
alienated and non-alienated voters rather than into the
customary categories of Democrats, Republicans, Independents, Protestants, Catholics, etc."; he claims that the
"alienated voter whose disillusionment with both parties
is great is the most significant independent." In *The Com-*

pleat Politician (a recently published study written in collaboration with Mr. George Blackwood) Professor Levin lays out model lines of strategy for the capture of the man who has "abandoned his traditional party loyalties." The immediate objectives of the strategy are to effect an identification of the candidate himself "with the alienated voter" (this the candidate accomplishes "by stressing his own powerlessness"), and "to intensify the feelings of powerlessness" among voters (this the candidate accomplishes by "emphasizing the unchecked tyranny of the incumbents and intimating that their hegemony is the cause of the citizen's powerlessness"). The particular quality needed by the managers of such campaigns is described as "creative cynicism." The gambits favored are various. They include reliance upon "opinion polls" (substitutes for formal speeches) in which voters are asked to give their views—while the questioner subtly implants, through the questions themselves, views favorable to his candidate; paid political broadcasts in the form of objective news reports, which appear "to be unsponsored and non-political and may therefore [seem] more credible to alienated voters"; advertisements that put a case for one party as opposed to another—but in terms negative enough to persuade skeptics. Professor Levin notes: "During the Ward-Volpe contest [for the Governorship in 1960] an advertising executive who had been advising candidates in Massachusetts for thirty years suggested to an influential Republican that his party could take advantage of feelings of political powerlessness among the electorate by placing the following advertisement in newspapers throughout the state:

'Negroes
Jews
Protestants
excluded from participation
in
the Democratic Party.' "

The suggestion was not followed—for technical as opposed to moral reasons.

The connection between the formulas thus summarized
and the old theory of political image-building are evident. Much has been written on the theme of the attractive
candidate as the political mute—a set of gestures, a figure
in a myth, a man capable of asking his audience to look
straight into his heart for solutions to community problems (solutions that take the form of lessons in likableness
and decency). But there *is* a further stage implicit in the
"politics of alienation." In campaigns conducted in accordance with the assumptions of this politics, every
candidate is an outsider, every candidate is obliged to
avoid subjects requiring the use of any outright political
language, indeed every candidate is required to *abuse*
such subjects—because acceptance of obligations to a
party organization amounts to evidence of black turpitude.
The minor paradoxes that multiply in such contests need
no gloss: the man seeking party endorsement secures it
by declaring his scorn for it; the politician seeking paid
political office secures it by noisily despising people who
depend on politics "for a living." But beyond lies the less
palpable truth that uninterrupted exposure to campaigns
organized on this model means the formalization of a

whole new area of taboo. As the long democratic struggle to replace suspicion of governors with confidence in
them is given over, politics itself, the organization of
public life, emerges as an ultimate unspeakable of human
experience.

The latter vision leads away, of course, from present
truths; it is proper to acknowledge that, when considered
in isolation, the new politics visible at the Massachusetts
conventions stirs something less than hysteria. The recent
conventions did not create the trend toward party apolitics, and the intensity of the effort at Springfield to draw
upon the reservoir of popular suspicion of the politician
was hardly unprecedented. Only two years ago the Democratic Convention was harassed by charges (comparable
to those made by Mr. McCormack) that one candidate
had in effect bought the conclave, by providing hotel
rooms for scores of delegates, meals for hundreds, and
promises of jobs for an uncounted number. The author of
the charges, no longer a prominent figure, was Robert F.
Murphy, known as "Mr. Integrity"; the man accused,
Joseph Ward, turned up in 1962 as a candidate for the
Attorney Generalship. And this season it was his turn to
present himself as the apolitical outsider, the new "Mr.
Integrity." (Mr. Ward's flyers described him as a "Lawyer-
Educator-Author," and his "personal platform" included
a plank calling for the creation of a "twenty [20] man
'Baby FBI' implemented by 'untouchables' " to fight cor-
ruption; he was defeated for the convention endorsement
by Rocky Marciano's highschool chum.) Roles, in short,

are played and exchanged from year to year—and at no time in the history of elective office has the part of the underdog been without attractions.

Yet, returning to the point of moment, there is at least one compelling reason (in Massachusetts at any rate) for *not* considering the evidences of apolitical politics in isolation—namely, the extraordinarily urgent local need for a confrontation with specific party problems. As indicated at the outset, the condition of Democratic party organization in Massachusetts is appalling enough to have roused a group of much-admired party members to full-scale action aimed at its repair. Insofar as the party chaos becomes a handmaid to official corruption, it is a matter of importance to every resident of the state. Responsible proposals for meeting the problem have been framed. Candidates for office have been asked to declare themselves on these proposals. It is in this context that the reluctance of the candidate to speak forthrightly as a party man—a politician well schooled, a figure with a relish for the intricacies of organization that alone bring power and discipline into being—deserves to be considered. And when the reluctance *is* thus considered, the ground for concern about the movement toward apoliticality seems anything but trivial.

To voice this concern is not to suggest that the vitality of party life as social exchange is disappearing. Neither clichés nor bad cigars hide the fact that state political conventions remain archetypal expressions of human solidarity. The scene is all heartiness unfeigned; merry greetings, shouting handshakes. Laughter bursts forth con-

tinually at old ones that have stood the test of time—
"So after Michael tells the magistrate he didn't hit her, he
never hits his wife, the magistrate turns around and he
says kind of nice: 'Now Nellie, will you tell us your side,
won't you," and right away Mike says, 'Oh for God's
sakes, Your Honor, don't listen to her. She's punch-
drunk!' " There is rueful warm communion at the moment
of defeat—in the "hospitality suites" of the men whose
"pledged" delegates were treacherously departing, deep-
bosomed, full-cheeked, moist-eyed ladies in hair nets and
print dresses sit on window sills in the half-light, drinking
quietly, nearly enjoying the unspoken concord of loyalty,
the rich shared wisdom of loss. Nor should it be thought
that the forces of the Commonwealth Organization of
Democrats left the convention empty-handed. The approved state party platform was an admirable document—
clear in its recommendations on tax policy, firm in its
positions on administrative reform—and no influence on
the draftsmen was greater than that of COD.

But it does finally have to be said that clarity about the
virtues of constitutional reform or governmental reor-
ganization or the graduated income tax is neither more
valuable nor more urgent than clarity about the virtues
of town and ward committees as opposed to the one-man
organizations that choke them off, or than clarity about
the virtues of open party finances or open scrutiny of
patronage—indeed of every device that toughens the
faith of political man in his own potency. Doubtless few
are unaware that if politics becomes the unmentionable,
power and hypocrisy will be one; probably many are

aware that the struggle for politics proper cannot much longer be postponed. But at the Massachusetts conclaves last summer this awareness itself seemed a dirty little secret, and as yet the "Commonwealth" still awaits the proud believable champion of the cause.

1962

America Absolved

For saints and seers History is all one: they call it terror (Eliade) or nightmare (Joyce) or inertia (Nietzsche) and dream of escape. For lesser men, though, the matter is complicated. Aware of history as an oppressive dead hand on experience, they think of it also as a contrivance, that which historians make or "do," and they tend to be optimistic about the doings. Shrewd inquirers can find things out about the past that, as the historian Marc Bloch says, the past didn't know about itself, or didn't wish to know. They also can learn forgotten languages, social or political, which, used with appropriate gingerliness as a means of interpreting the present, win respect for critiques of contemporary dogma that would seem outrageous if delivered in contemporary terms. Neither accomplishment enables the inquirer to get the full weight of the monkey-past off his back; neither offers the audience a ready way up and out of time into eternity—that for which seers have a crying need. But both provide people with release in the form of a glimpse of Now from the outside. And in a faithless age the need for this release is so great that whatever satisfies it deserves regard as a kind of poor man's grace.

As should at once be admitted, commonplaces like these are irrelevant to ordinary works of American history. Most studies of our past are written by men who are simply passing respectably through the professional day, harming nobody, keeping facts in sight, establishing that the humble act of being *sound* about any subject demands hard work (the point can never be well-enough established).

And at first glance Richard Hofstadter's recent treatise on brains in America appears to deserve no higher praise than this. The tenth book of a forty-six-year-old scholar, *Anti-Intellectualism in American Life* (1963) promises little to people who read professional tomes for the pleasure of encountering (or imagining) appurtenances of the lost world of leisure—library loafers, claret lunches, fireside teas, pretty calligraphy, and the like. A whiff of grimy worldliness, essence of textbook–TV–time-study academia, rises from its pages; some provincial readers who turn them will call to mind the stereotype of the Columbia prof as the proprietor of a madly expanding one-man insurance brokerage—a hustler nailing the big premium every time he hits the street, quoting rates in phone booths while nibbling a desperate Nab, shooting back to the shop to break in a fleet of new clerks and stenographers

(the staff Dean Barzun said every professor should have),
and all the while flogging himself with the dream of getting out early tonight to Bellmore to spend half an hour
with the kids. The author announces that he worked on
and off at this large volume for ten years; in that period he
delivered lectures in series at a splendid variety of other institutions (the universities of Michigan and Southern
California, Hiram College, Smith College, Princeton—
and Cambridge, overseas), wheeled and dealed success-
fully with the foundations (the Carnegie Corporation and
the Fund for the Advancement of Education were among
his supporters), and finished *six* other books. His thanks
go forth to no fewer than four "research assistants," a
Miss Gruber among them. Toward the close of his book
he delivers himself on the natural isolation of the intellectual ("The truly creative mind is hardly ever so alone
as when it is trying to be sociable. . . . Facing the world
. . . alone seems to be the characteristic creative
stance"), and a page or two later he acknowledges the
help not only of the four assistants but of thirty-three
friends. And throughout he abides by the noxious footnote rules which require an academic author to drop off at
the bottom of every page, like a young mouser mewing
pridefully at the back door, a furry little ball of dead ad-
jectival tribute. ("Marcus Cunliffe, in his penetrating
study . . ." "Merle Curti, in his suggestive little volume
. . ." "For an excellent statement about the numbers
. . . see Timothy L. Smith. . . ." "For an interesting ex-
ercise in definition, see Morton White. . . ." "For a
spirited defense and appreciation . . . see Samuel Eliot

Morison. . . ." "For a stimulating exploration . . . see R. W. B. Lewis. . . ." Etc.)

Nor is it merely superficies and trivia of production and composition that raise doubts about the book's essential value. No one before Professor Hofstadter had thought to write a history of American attitudes toward mind, tracing general cycles of hatred, love, and apathy from the seventeenth century to the present, and avoiding such pitfall topics as "highbrow anti-rationalism." But few specialists in any period of the American past have left these attitudes wholly out of account—which is to say that the "field" of anti-intellectualism is not one from which news for professional Americanists can easily be reaped. Professor Hofstadter treats patterns of intellectualism and anti-intellectualism in religion (from the Puritan clergy through the Awakeners and Evangelicals to the evolution controversy), in politics (from the decline of the Federalist elite through Godkin and the Civil Service reformers to the rise of the expert), in business ("the vanguard of anti-intellectualism in our culture"), and in education (special attention to Dewey and the gospel of life adjustment). The heroes, episodes, and books that figure in his most entertaining pages—Davy Crockett, Henry Adams in Washington, Billy Sunday, George Washington Plunkitt of Tammany, Carnegie, Vanderbilt, T. R. as "fighting intellectual," Robert M. La Follette, the Scopes Trial, the Brain Trust, Henry C. Link's *The Return to Religion,* Adlai Stevenson—have been heard of before. The evidence marshaled in support of his perceptions often amounts only to a long paraphrase of one or another recent, readily available study. (Professor Hofstadter was startled, presumably while reading Daniel Aaron's *Writers on the Left* [1961], by the continuity between traditional business attitudes toward mind and those appearing in leftist discourse of the 1920's and 1930's. He pieces out this "insight" for seven anecdotal paragraphs in which every quotation and incident, as the footnote brightly reports, is taken "from [Aaron], pp. 25, 41, 65, 93-4, 132n, 162, 163-4, 168, 209, 210-212, 216, 227, 240-2, 254, 308, 337-8, 346, 409, 410, 417, 425.") And impatience, a force that occasionally pushes him toward melodrama and away from analysis, seems least well controlled precisely when he approaches the subjects—the psychology of the elitist withdrawal in the 1820's, for one—that he is best placed to probe.

That in spite of these failings *Anti-Intellectualism in American Life* does succeed in recovering a forgotten language is owing largely to the author's ease with complexity, his readiness to present the brain-baiting of the past in its full socio-political context. "To be confronted with a simple and unqualified evil is no doubt a kind of luxury," says Professor Hofstadter at the outset, "but such is not the case here; and if anti-intellectualism has become, as I believe it has, a broadly diffused quality in our civilization, it has become so because it has often been linked to good, or at least defensible, causes." The position has shortcomings, of course: the writer's fondness for qualification and distaste for moralizing fervor prevent the neglected truth which he brings back into view from becoming the center of a passionate argument. Alienated waifs and moony hipsters on the one hand, Establishment

apologists on the other, will be piqued—but not shaken—
by his words; ordinary folk will perceive the fatuity of
some modern assumptions about "the situation of the intellectual" without being released from their weight. Yet,
as these remarks imply, materials for a powerful critique
of contemporary cant lie at hand for the reader of *Anti-
Intellectualism,* and at those moments when the author
puts them to effective use, the book rises to the level of a
major project of reclamation.

The neglected truth reclaimed, namely that one man's
anti-intellectualism is another man's democratic aspiration, is well represented in the opening chapters, which explain with admirable clarity why simplicity needs to be
laid by:

[Anti-intellectualism] first got its strong grip on our ways of
thinking because it was fostered by an evangelical religion
that also purveyed many humane and democratic sentiments.
It made its way into our politics because it became associated
with our passion for equality. It has become formidable in
our education partly because our educational beliefs are
evangelically egalitarian. Hence, as far as possible, our anti-
intellectualism must be excised from the benevolent impulses
upon which it lives by constant and delicate acts of intellectual
surgery which spare these impulses themselves. Only in this
way can anti-intellectualism be checked and contained; I do
not say eliminated altogether, for I believe not only that this
is beyond our powers but also that an unbridled passion for
the total elimination of this or that evil can be as dangerous as
any of the delusions of our time.

But the force of the truth in question stems less from the
flat statements of the author than from the language of

the past that he quotes. For it is this language—some of
it spoken by the elite, some by the unwashed—which
puts the reader in fresh touch with the complicated, even
dignified, feelings for which the historian offers his defense.

In the elite voices, dignity is sometimes the concomitant
of a kind of humane pastoral generosity, as when Jeffer-
son contrasts the moral sense of the ploughman with that
of the professor. (The contrast, favorable to the ploughman, is made in terms altogether free of the vices of self-
hatred or sentimentality that now unman some men of
mind.) And sometimes it is a product of the habit of
responsibility, as when Greeley remarks that the reason
the American yeoman wavers in his natural respect for
talent and learning is that talent and learning are too often "directed to the acquisition of wealth and luxury by
means which add little to the aggregate of human com-
forts, and rather subtract from his own special share of
them." The voices of the unwashed, in contrast, can be
respected because they are rooted, as Greeley implies, in
a real world—one in which men who cry out against Establishment selfishness are responding to fact not fantasy,
and are moved by commendable aspiration for their sons,
not by *ressentiment*. The North Billerica, Mass., farmer
whose anti-intellectual, anti-Establishment pamphlet called
The Key of Libberty appeared in 1798 was, as Professor Hofstadter admits, a crude man, unworried about
"the consequence of his policy for high culture"—but he
was no enthusiast of ignorance. His paper opened with the
assertion that "Learning & Knowledge is essential to the
preservation of Libberty & unless we have more of it

amongue us we Cannot Seporte our Libertyes Long." The
point of the man's attack on physicians, ministers, judges,
and "all letirary men & the over grown rich" is that their
single concern is to elevate the status of the professions:

. . . the few are always crying up the advantages of costly
collages, national acadimyes and gramer schooles, in order to
make places for men to live without work and so strengthen
their party. But are always opposed to cheep schooles &
woman schooles, the ondly or prinsaple means by which larn-
ing is spred amongue the Many. . . . For if we apply for a
Preacher or a School Master, we are told the price. So Much,
& they can't go under, for it is agreed upon & they shall be
disgrased if they take less.

And the historian, reviewing this charge in the light of
conditions of the age—"a time when the vaunted common school system of Massachusetts was being neglected"
—is obliged to assert that "there was a certain rough justice in [it that] cannot be denied."

As already indicated, *Anti-Intellectualism in American
Life* has other ends in view besides the pursuit of "rough
justice" on this model. Professor Hofstadter's decision
about the North Billerica farmer is that his position was
ultimately damaging to "intellectual culture." He takes
the same view of the NEA and the gospel of life adjustment, of Charles Grandison Finney and "Presbygational"
evangelism, and (at a lower level) of Cotton Ed Smith,
who told the Senate that Rex Tugwell was unqualified to
be Undersecretary of Agriculture because he had never
been a dirt farmer, hence was "not a graduate of God's
Great University." At no point does he become an apologist for sunny mindlessness. But at every moment he is

conscious that in a democratic society effort to apply fixed labels to men in the name of mind or of taste is unrealistic: whom the elite call vulgar are also to be called brother, the unwashed are also the unadvantaged, the unrealized are never, flatly, the unredeemable. "It is rare for an American intellectual," says Professor Hofstadter, "to confront candidly the unresolvable conflict between the elite character of his own class and his democratic aspirations." And it is largely because, in conducting his historical inquiries, he himself rarely shies from such confrontations that his book arrives repeatedly at hitherto inexpressible truths. He succeeds in defining psycho-political implications of the contemporary intellectual's fascination with mass culture—estrangement from democratic faith among them. ("The . . . note of inhumanity, which often creeps into discussions of mass culture may be explained in some part by an underlying sense of grievance against a populace that has not lived up to expectations.") And addressing himself to deeper convictions of the same men, he is able to name the precise shift of assumption that in recent days has driven intellectuals on toward extravagance and cant:

The prophets of alienation who speak for the left no doubt aim to create a basis for some kind of responsible politics of protest, but when the situation of the intellectual is under consideration their tone becomes strident, and then one hears how much better it is to have "blind unreasoning rejection" rather than to make moral compromises; the talk is of nostalgia for "earlier certainties that made resistance easy," of the primary need of the intellectual to discharge aggression, of the dangers of becoming a "prostitute" or a "traitor" to the fundamental obligations of the intellectual's role, of the alleged antithesis between social responsibility, which is bad, and intellectual responsibility, which is good. The point here is that alienation in the intellectual is not simply accepted, as a necessary consequence of the pursuit of truth or of some artistic vision, but that a negative stance or posture toward society is prescribed as the only stance productive of artistic creativity or social insight or moral probity.

Regrettably, those likely to be hostile to Professor Hofstadter's account of the cult of alienation are offered a weapon by the range of his book's backward glance. The very orthography of the key texts cited suggests that intense democratic aspiration, perfervid labor toward self-realization, belong to the past. Yes, yes, in olden times scholars and artists and professionals were abused in large part because they seemed determined to prevent others from rising to their rank. But what of the last two decades? Why does the learned professor not deal directly with Hiss-Chambers or with the McCarthy years? If he had focused on these episodes would he have found it possible to establish a relation between anti-intellectualism and "humane and democratic sentiments"? Would he still have believed in the appropriateness (in a mass society) of talk about excising anti-intellectualism from benevolent impulses "by delicate acts of intellectual surgery"? Isn't it a fact that the professor makes his case by avoiding the grittiest episodes in memory—outbursts that did incomparably more damage to "intellectual culture" than any he cites?

The questions are not trivial, and they cannot be answered by mere assertions that the anti-Establishment

furies of the late forties and mid-fifties are themselves as
complex in origin as any released in the nineteenth century. (The critique of contemporary dogma does indeed
seem outrageous when delivered in contemporary terms.)
Still there is some point in recalling that only a few years
before these furies occurred Americans had undergone an
experience of hierarchical rigor which may well have
been for millions stunning in its effect. The voice of
privilege and command of those days spoke often in a
tone controlled more by sniffishness than by manly love
of the flag, or by the sense of necessities of discipline, and
nobody could have loved it. You will not eat our food,
wear our clothes, enter our clubs; you will not speak
until spoken to; you will sir, salute, or snivel to youth, in-
competence, even apparent stupidity: for you are not a
college man. Had the Harvard lieutenants and Bowdoin
ensigns tipped a universal wink, "military courtesy"
would have disappeared and doubtless military discipline
as well; but millions would have had a less exacerbating
encounter with "trained minds." What was taught by the
educated gentlemen whose land and beeves were leaves
and bars wasn't manners alone but the very concept of
establishmentarianism, exclusiveness itself. And how content were these lecturers, many of them brave men, how
extraordinarily untormented in their separateness! How
remarkably comfortable (for them) the transition from
the rhetoric of equality to the rhetoric of superiors and
inferiors! In the glance of brass-browed military man there
was that which probably chilled countless dreams of mobility and self-realization. And conceivably the resentment
and frustration thus amassed—anger at university smug-

ness known at first hand—wasn't an insignificant part of the huge capital drawn on by mind-baiters in the Hiss and McCarthy years.

Does it follow from this that the events of those years, the release of rage in persecution, re-created democratic faith in America? Some who read these words will not scorn that conclusion. There were schoolboys going off to work in the middle and late thirties, while others were enthroned as freshmen, who learned to envy the rich and the lucky, and sustained themselves on a smelly broth of feeling—self-pity, no hope for the ambitious, BOYS BOYS BOYS in the back-page agency ads of the *Herald Trib*— that was the staple too of the soldier's life. And there are a few who have acknowledged that the great upheaval of 1947, the tearing down of the Ivy by the grocer's boy from Whittier, meant something: *they* could be turned on, the lucky ones, *they* did not own the world. . . . The present writer, a reporter, husband, father, and vet in his mid-twenties then, found satisfaction for his ignorance in the baying of that elite; he remembers to his shame (the latter a belated achievement) that the episode encouraged him in his "decision" to turn student.

And while there are limits to the personal reference, they are not so overpowering as to cancel the relevant possibility—namely that any moment in American life at which men of ordinary intelligence and powerful desire believe themselves to be blocked off, anti-intellectualism is likely to become impure: a mode for the release of decent aspiration as well as of vicious, mindless envy. To think of that discovery as absolution (everything understood, everything forgiven) is, to be sure, to become a victim of history on the model Nietzsche described. But to think of it as a further snippet telling on Professor Hofstadter's "side," supporting arguments for a complicated understanding of anti-intellectualism, might be neither a hopeless error nor an invitation to complacency. It is true that the great American trick of yesteryear was that of being oblivious to the defects of virtues—but presently the trick is that of being oblivious to the virtues of defects. And both tricks cheat. Never in England, say some, could a McCarthy terrorize academies, politicians, best people: there the challenge would be despised. But the weakness here that could not despise, that could only trim and whine and hide, was at least a human villainy—evidence that in America men charged as figures of privilege are incapable of retaining their equipoise, can actually be shamed for lighting each other's candles, paying out to members only the soft jobs, the easy chairs, the solid cots, the whiskey in the rest area, the ham-and-jam breakfasts, the coffee and buns at Battalion. And that shame is a potency as well as a disaster.

To repeat: the reassertion of connections between mind-baiting and democratic aspiration creates no ground for self-congratulation, no wholly satisfactory vocabulary of grace. The writer who takes up the task of studying the links cannot think of himself as engaged in producing a work that the community of knowledge will welcome as a necessary book. And it is possible—despite truisms about the uses of history—that the author of *Anti-Intellectualism in American Life* would have contributed more had he dared to face the chaos in memory. The result of his labor, though, is far from another piece of production-line Americana: courageously sane at its best, the book demands praise as a work which not only serves truth and the nation simultaneously, but erects a new barrier against despair.

1963

Character
of the
Assassin

He knew nobody and nobody knew him. What he was after, at the beginning as at the end, was a sign—a word from Out There, to acknowledge his difference, his specialness. But before the first hint reached him (from New York, on party stationery), there were terrible silences and several bad blows.

Some of the blows can be numbered: No hero's spot in the backfield. He was fast, loved to hit, but nature, weighing him lightly, picked him for "B" teams. No job with a title. In a world in which work is the only "socialization" and socialization the only salvation, he had no mastered technique, no low-number slot on the plant bowling team, no lunch-hour appointments with a personally interested aide in the department of human engineering, hence no on-the-job redemption.

The right uniform offered a chance. As the Navy was better than the Army, so the Marines were better than both. But once a Marine there you were again: the others, as it developed, were also Marines.

A second language, foreignness itself, seemed promising —choose Russian, a shocker. But once a Russian there you were again: the Russians were overworked and overwatched, and only turned up their hands.

Love was well regarded. He tried an imprisonment by marriage. He bore a smiling innocent away from those who spoke her language, the better to insure the absoluteness of her need. But then in the customs shed in New York there was someone waiting by his luggage, a Travelers Aid man speaking Russian to his wife. And then Texas produced, from nowhere, for her, a *cercle russe*. And then, although still manacled in his glassy charm, she herself drove a lance into his "love": the alien bride, his dependent, taught herself to say "Hello."

At every moment politics beckoned. But the sequel proved time and time again that, in his sense, there was no politics—no prize ring of argument from which a gutsy little guy, able in debate to knock over any number of Birching patsies, could jump up overnight into the Congressional big time. In Moscow, Mexico City, North Dakota, New Orleans, in the Corps, in the Bronx, there was only fuzz and more fuzz, an administrative wall, government as a cool promoter.

The resources of fantasy were endless. A scrapper and an expatriate and a hunter, he was therefore a writer, therefore entitled to compare himself with "E. Hemingway." (The letter naming his grievance and proposing the comparison to the Governor, then Secretary of the Navy, had but a single misspelled word.) Later he was a counter-agent, equipped with beard and gun. Still later he found comfort in an assumed name with a reserved patrician sigh in its sound: A. Hydell, A. Hidell. But within the soft blur of the name, fantasy selves whirled like the blades of a fan. (Hydell, Hidell: hide, hell, hideous, idle, idol, Fidel, Hyde, Jekyll . . .) The unbearable problem with fantasy was that sooner or later characters in it began devouring each other.

The best course led toward knowledge. Be informed. Study. In the chaos of print seek a coherence. Write. Periodically he turned in this direction, and, toward the end, we see him on a New Orleans porch, reading "all day long"—newspapers, magazines, books from the public library. Marxism pro and con. And, for a change of pace, adventures in governor-gunning. He frightens his landlord with his bookish jag, and, a fast reader, makes other real progress. He finds his way freshly, learns to anticipate criticism and head off objections. Already he can argue with an *aircraft engineer,* beat the man to the phrase evening after evening, almost embarrassing. Nor is it just this chap who sees his stuff. New York too, on the printed stationery. What a moment for an opening in textbooks to appear!

But once more there is a problem. The job isn't right. Maintenance again. He is *carrying* books, lugging cartons. Quick hands, quick mind, world traveler, two languages, radio debater, author, spells dialectic and other hard words—this is the way up? Senator Fidel Hemingway a slavey? Bastards! Nigger-bombers! Pricks! The whirling begins—New York, the party, Huey, the Marines, Robert Jordan, the hunter. His memory falling apart, idle Fidel returns to the Louisiana fantasy, but plans the raid in earnest. From the top of the mountain. Eating a reconnoitered chicken on the side of the hill with his mates, he shoots the infiltrators and then—grace under pressure— laughs aloud, bravely, with his fellow comrades who have commandeered a bus in the city streets. And here at last *is* the echo, on its way unblocked, enormous in the tiled tunnel, lights, cries—calling him by some other name but still calling him. And here too as usual is the enemy, familiarly behatted and white-shirted, lunging for him, crushing his belly. Screaming, Hydell down for the count hears his name again, the last words in his ears—"you son of a bitch."

Vermin, wretch, madman, sneerer—these and worse are the names by which this man has since been known. They are at once useful and useless terms. They release feeling, but, like the interminable sermons on "responsibility" (who bears it? left? right? left? right?), they fail to raise relevant questions. Some of the latter are: how many similar men—unsocialized, anomic, workless—survive? Are their opposites all "safe"? Is it true that the completely socialized man, the viewer and voter who has work, a kindly oblivion—is it a fact that this man can be counted upon to maintain himself? Finally: can a few decades of such self-maintenance be called a human life?

The task of bringing these questions alive into the public consciousness seems on its face insuperable. Thus far thinkers only, not doers, have conceded their urgency.

(Among these "thinkers," as may as well be added, have been far too many figures of bombast, apocalyptic buffoons.) Few believed that the dead President, himself a pragmatist, a tough customer, would one day venture to address such matters. City and Country wits alike knew him as a minuteman trapped in immediacies, taxes, deterrents, and NATO. ". . . I cannot think of a single person in high public office whom many intelligent persons regard with deep respect," says a writer in the issue of the *New York Review* that lies at hand. And where was the evidence to disprove this standard line? An odd eye for dark lines in a newly lionized poet. Adeptness at grasping unlovely tangles in the motives of giving men, "selfless contributors to the public weal." (Self-love, nothing finer, said the President, propelled the Adams family.) A witty protective manner, an inclination to yield only a piece of himself to audiences—the mark of a man who has met his own torment and believes in the reality of troubles that do not meet the eye. And above the rest: readiness to pretend that a tentative step toward complication—toward diversity as a value—might be possible in public discourse.

In sum: bits and snippets. This writer, who matters not at all, learns (doubtless with others) that he had pinned his hope to these snippets. To a fantasy that after eight years of pragmatics, eight years in which personal beauty, physical vibrancy, relish and competence at the urgencies of doers had established him as the only voice of the nation, there would come, in the Kennedy retirement, a turn to a new subject—the American character, the need for a defense of humanness as distinguished from the defense of humanity. Awareness of the need wouldn't do wonders, but couldn't fail to help. An intermediary between the genuine two cultures—men who think, men who do—was essential to its creation. There were but three requirements for the position: mind, capacity for balancing concern for others with knowledge that such concern is indeed "unnatural," immense personal attractiveness that encourages the audience to listen. And the murdered Chief had them all.

Whether real or fancied, that chance is gone. The task of defending "free institutions" and the task of preserving the naturalness and wholeness this defense imperils return, even for the fantast, to their separateness. Assurances have been given: "policy" will not change, a campaign against name-calling is to be mounted, the Outdoor Advertising Council promises its aid. But this remains a bad moment. If the dead President did not yet know his assassin, he did possess mind enough to find him out. It isn't easy to believe that the future will quickly announce a winner with a better chance of learning A. Hydell's real and fearful name.

November 24, 1963

Project for
Another
Country

Society normally asks little or nothing of [the American intellectual without connections]; a reform situation, on the other hand, seems to present him with a role. Yet even here the only pressures exerted on him involve the maintenance of a steady stream of new and exciting ideas; his only measurement of effect must be that of audience appeal; his principal question must continue to be, How many are listening? The pressures he does not feel are the concrete demands of an institution as such; he feels no direct responsibility for a clientele; he has, in short, no vested interest. The result for the intellectual is a situation of no limits. His reform thinking will tend to be erratic, emotional, compulsive, and abstract.

Stanley Elkins, SLAVERY *(1959)*

That the project won few unguarded good words, either from venturesome types who inspected its Harlem premises (a community center on West 137th Street near

Lenox Avenue), or from viewers from afar, seemed on its face puzzling.

The Congressional act that underwrote it had been loudly hailed by leaders of both parties at the time of its passage in 1961. (The act empowered the Secretary of Health, Education and Welfare to grant federal subsidies to privately initiated programs that "hold promise of making a substantial contribution to the prevention or control of juvenile delinquency.") The projectors' idea—that of organizing a "Domestic Peace Corps" whose members would serve for a year as "aides" in Harlem's understaffed welfare agencies—was modest and sensible. Volunteers had been recruited, details of their placement had been arranged, and an intelligent training program was under way—one that offered instruction in the skills of the social worker as well as in relevant history and sociology. The founders had coordinated their effort with that of the only major youth agency functioning in the area, and had secured recognition from City Hall—in the form of commitments to provide medical care, in municipal hospitals, for the volunteers. And, in addition, they had advanced beyond the maze of practical problems to frame a conceptual definition of their goals (drawing on role psychology, and on the studies of "delinquency subcultures" made by Richard Cloward and Lloyd Ohlin, it envisioned the college-educated Negro volunteers both as "supplementary welfare personnel" and as "role models" for Harlem youth in the large). Final assessment of the project was, obviously, a matter for the future. But the fact of its existence, an independent, coherent enterprise in what is called self-help, amounted to fresh evidence that resources of leadership in the American Negro community were no longer negligible. And the likelihood appeared strong that this evidence would arouse a positive response.

As should be said at once, the failure of the likelihood to materialize wasn't equally mysterious in all quarters. Innocence, which believes among other things in the possibility of a federal grant without political dimensions, could not approve an award of two hundred and fifty thousand dollars to Harlem: the latter is Representative Adam Clayton Powell's territory and there are several points of connection between the project and the legislator. (The connections, none of them damning, were traced in fury by Senator John Williams of Delaware and the columnist Drew Pearson; questioned about them, the director of the project—a sharp lawyer named Livingston Wingate—commented dryly that the DPC would increase the Congressman's local stature only if "cleanly conducted," and added that there were other reasons beside this for "not letting the project be touched.") And officials of the "real" Peace Corps had a fair complaint— arising out of problems in nomenclature. The founders of the Domestic Peace Corps had appropriated that title with brio but without sanction, and were still using it in a manner that blurred distinctions. The confusion became nearly impenetrable after the President's message to Congress of February 14, which recommended the creation of a "National Service Corps" and a "Youth Conservation Corps" (the former is often referred to in the press as the "Domestic Peace Corps").

For the rest, there were murmurings that no group of thirty to thirty-five young men and women could hope to alter a world as seriously disadvantaged as Central Harlem—an area without a single public high school, cursed with the highest rates of delinquency (and addiction) in the country and the lowest personal incomes (on the average) in the city. And the scene itself, of course, was no richer in promise, or in hints of aspiration, than were the statistics. The routes traversed by the volunteers and staff members on their way to and from P.S. 100, the Abraham Lincoln Community Center, the Joseph P. Kennedy, Jr., Memorial Center, and other destinations lead past grocery windows that advertise kingfish, coons, and

> Turkey tips
>> necks
>> wings,

and past mocking side-street idlers ("How you doing, Buddy? Hey, Buddy, you go to college, Buddy? Hey Buddy, you go to City College? Hey, Buddy, how you doing?") DPC headquarters itself, a drab building attached to the foot of a beaten brownstone row, bears a wall-bolted notice of grim non-welcome (NO LOITERING OR BALLPLAYING). And the nearly decrepit rooms within, which house the male volunteers as well as remnants of an older community-center tradition (a beauty parlor among them) are redolent of hair-wave fluid, a scent highly nourishing to gloom.

But even in the context of "probable impact" the decision to rest in gloom seemed perverse. A pattern for the enlargement of enterprises like the Corps has been laid down (the hierarchy ascends from "planning grants" to "training and action grants" to "demonstration grants"), and the organizers of the Corps were following it closely. They made known to the volunteers that theirs was a "pilot project," and that the aim was not to transform Harlem but to build a record on which to base applications for larger grants; proof that small beginnings of this sort could issue in projects of indisputably significant scope was available in the history of the twelve-and-a-half-million-dollar Mobilization For Youth program on New York's Lower East Side. Almost to a man, moreover, the outside observers who bothered to notice the DPC were themselves familiar not only with the "structure" of welfare grants but with political reality—which is to say, they possessed knowledge that ought to have inhibited pessimism. But, as indicated, this knowledge had small effect: hostile writers spoke openly of the possibility of scandal, friendly writers adopted attitudes which DPC staff members described, disappointedly, as "ironical and sarcastic." (The soundest of the reports, by Murray Kempton in the *New Republic,* spoke of the program as "an accident," claimed that the grant had been made "for all the wrong reasons," and suggested that the best that could be said for the Corps was that "the lives of these particular children [the volunteers] will never be exactly the same again.") The plain case was that even men of mind and known good will felt obliged to resist any impulse to enthusiasm. And, since the projectors' labors would undoubtedly be evaluated in part according to their success in exciting public support, questions about the ultimate source of this resistance had an edge of urgency as well as of interest.

The notion, pedantic at first glance, that a search for the source requires some attention to history gains force when differences between the DPC and other attacks on "problems of Negroes" are brought into focus. The chief difference is that the Domestic Peace Corps addresses itself to these problems not with moral or juridical abstractions but in situational (or cultural) terms. Effort elsewhere takes shape as a struggle to guarantee legal rights or to show forth anti-Negro prejudice as evil. Here the labor is to understand Negro personality in its relation to a particular cultural setting, and to attempt to change that relation with the aim of altering basic patterns of character.

The currently accepted account of patterns of character in Harlem youth is, as would be expected, simple in its essentials. It stresses the sense of entrapment—that which, as Messrs. Cloward and Ohlin argue in their *Delinquency and Opportunity* (1960), controls behavior wherever institutional modes of the way up and out are lacking:

. . . many lower-class male adolescents experience desperation born of the certainty that their position in the economic structure is relatively fixed and immutable—a desperation made all the more poignant by their exposure to a cultural ideology in which failure to orient oneself upward is regarded as a moral defect and failure to become mobile as proof of it.

One way of countering or at least easing the desperation is to establish early on the immediacy of the relation between schooling and mobility ("some youths become hoodlums . . . not because they lack the ability to succeed legitimately . . . but because they find out too late the relationship between school adjustment and [upward social mobility]"). And it is with this end in mind that the DPC assigns a volunteer—a poised attractive student from Southern University at Baton Rouge, La., named Mildred Love—to P.S. 100, the local elementary school. Miss Love's task is to assist in organizing a pre-school clinic for parents of first-graders. The purpose of the clinic is to initiate talk in pleasant circumstances between parents and teachers, thereby creating school as a reality—a place which, if treated earnestly by the family as well as the pupil, can have as considerable an effect upon the life of nearly any first-grader grown to adulthood as it visibly has had in Miss Love's. Implicit in the undertaking, naturally, is a conviction that only an educated Negro can contend against discrimination and ultimately contribute to the Negro cause. But at its center lies an appeal not to a sacred cause or to the sense of self-satisfaction or moral outrage, but to self-*dis*satisfaction and personal ambition.

And precisely here, as it seems, lies one root of the failure of the DPC projectors to win ardent backing among outsiders. American liberals have usually been impatient, suspicious, or contemptuous of versions of "the Negro problem" which emphasize Negro incapacities, or otherwise imply that second-class citizenship is not simply a function of white men's viciousness. Some writers of tact, to be sure, have managed to hold their audience while sketching these incapacities—but only by insisting (properly) that the latter are a direct result of cultural deprivation, and by avoiding (sometimes disingenuously) the question how juridical action can be expected to repair them. A historian of C. Vann Woodward's stature can direct his reader toward awareness that Negro leaders themselves helped to create the image of the "inferior being." (". . . in proposing the virtual retirement of the mass of Negroes from the political life of the South, and in stressing the humble and menial role that the race was to play," Woodward wrote in *The Strange Career of Jim Crow* [1955, 1957], Booker T. Washington produced "a submissive philosophy for the Negro that to some whites must have appeared an invitation to further aggression.") And implicit in every assessment of race relations this historian has made is a feeling for the necessity of naming the stages of the Negro's self-development:

Negroes played important roles in both reconstruction periods, but it is obvious that in the present movement they are vastly better equipped to defend themselves and advance their cause than were their newly emancipated, propertyless, and largely illiterate grandfathers and great-grandfathers. Negroes have already shown new capacities for leadership that have surprised their friends as well as their opponents. In the long run, it may be that their own resources will prove decisive in the contest.

But writers who approach closer to the subject of self-development have not found it easy to win a hearing. Stanley Elkins' *Slavery* (1959), an invaluable book, argued convincingly that the stereotype of the Negro slave (Sambo) was in fact no stereotype but a fair representation of the man in that age—since, as comparative studies of slave cultures indicated, infantilism was the only possible direction for character to take in the unique slave culture of nineteenth-century America. With this thesis in the foreground, Elkins went on to criticize the Abolitionists who, oblivious to the truth that "a man's humanity, such as he has, lies not in his naked essence but in his culture," promulgated the doctrine of instant equality ("Here is man," said Emerson, "and if you have man, black or white is an insignificance"). The reaction of historians was wary, perhaps in part because acceptance of such arguments meant sacrificing the simple vocabulary in which "racial problems" have ever been defined. And it is doubtful that many right-thinking liberals are even now prepared to make that sacrifice. The 1954 Supreme Court decision that reversed the "separate and equal" rule was followed by outbursts of abstract fury not much different in temper from those that preceded the Civil War. The suggestion that civic adequacy must remain the primary goal, the claim that biological treatises proving that no ethnic group is "inherently" inferior weren't of particular value in the situation at hand—these were cast out as finkery. Afloat on a self-inflating cushion of sentimental guilt, the white liberal made once more for the ultra position—one which asserted (to use words that Professor Elkins applied to the Abolitionists of the mid-nineteenth century) that:

. . . the question must be contemplated in terms untouched by expediency, untarnished by society's organic compromises, uncorrupted even by society itself. It was a problem of conscience. . . .

With all this in mind it becomes a shade easier to understand the lukewarm modern response to "reform thinking" which places its emphasis on Negro character as well as on white men's turpitude.

For full understanding, however, the eye of the observer needs also to consider the relation between such reform thinking and contemporary attitudes toward institutions. The Domestic Peace Corps, the Harlem Youth Program, the Philadelphia Tutoring Project—these and a number of other current undertakings are, as the handy jargon has it, institution-oriented. Each DPC volunteer works in and through a community center, a school, a hospital, a welfare agency, or a coherent neighborhood; each new venture—summer camps, programs of vocational guidance or "leadership training"—is founded within the existing institutional framework; the prime assumption is that for young minds the sight of a *usable* organization, the possibility of seeing one's life in a non-antipathetic relation to *any* institution, is bound to complicate syndromes of violence or retreatism. But this positive view of institutions is out of harmony with current opinion elsewhere.

In a sense, of course, American faith in institutions has been "in process of breaking down" at nearly every period of American history. It isn't entirely without interest for the present point, for example, that Professor Elkins, to speak once more of him, attributes the fervor of the Abolitionists to their remoteness from centers of organized power, and to the breakdown of such centers—the bar, the ministry, the political elite—during the 1830's. (At that hour, Elkins notes, the American was coming to possess a new system of values, individualistic in assumption, with which he could " 'question' society itself, that

very society which had made success possible and which
offered him his future.") But the parallel is of limited application: in the 1960's opinion-makers do not question
institutions, they despise them. Literary and other fashion
scolds the citizen and prizes the prophet; the conviction
grows that the money culture has poisoned every social,
political, or religious instrument; persistence in locating
the best hope for reform outside the naked individual
psyche is dismissed as puerility.

What is more, the voice of the Negro himself has taken
up these commonplaces—to a loud chorus of approbation.
Some speeches in the vein described have, admittedly, been
poorly received. The Black Muslim movement, which
awaits an Armageddon that will destroy the whole structure of "white Christian society," has still won no Congressional support for its secessionary program. (According to C. Eric Lincoln, author of *The Black Muslims in
America* [1962], the official Muslim proposal is as follows:
"[Negroes], as the descendants of slaves who had contributed so much to the making of America without compensation . . . should be given a separate territory—
'fertile and minerally rich'—which should be subsidized
by the Federal Government 'for the next twenty to twenty-
five years'—until the black nation is able to produce for its
own needs.") But James Baldwin, at this moment the best-
known Negro writer in the country, has written an account
of Muslim leaders and theories (it forms the middle
section of his famous "Letter from a Region of My Mind")
which, although critical in conclusion, is rarely less than
respectful in tone. And the response to the apocalyptic,

violently anti-institutional program for "reform" set forth by this writer in the same document put beyond doubt the intensity of public enthusiasm for the oracular mode of address to racial issues.

The essay in question, admirable in its opening pages for an evocation of the caged hours of a Harlem boyhood, was marked by imaginative relish of moments of destruction ("The Negroes of this country may never be able to rise to power, but they are very well placed to ring down the curtain on the American dream"), and by existentialist death-mongering ("It seems to me that one ought to rejoice in the *fact* of death—ought to decide to earn one's death by confronting with passion the conundrum of life"). The "problem," as understood by Mr. Baldwin, was a matter of psychodynamics, an item vision alone, not history, could fathom:

The white man's unadmitted—and apparently, to him, unspeakable—private fears and longings are projected onto the Negro. The only way he can be released from the Negro's tyrannical power over him is to consent, in effect, to become black himself, to become a part of that suffering and dancing country that he now watches wistfully from the heights of his lonely power and, armed with spiritual traveller's checks, visits surreptitiously after dark. How can one respect, let alone adopt, the values of people who do not, on any level whatever, live the way they say they do, or the way they say they should?

While Mr. Baldwin repeatedly reviled the hypocrisy of Christians, he did not reach the rhetorical pitch of William Lloyd Garrison, who a century ago was nominating Jesus

Christ for the Presidency of the United States, and, as in the following passage, driving at his own pace toward Apocalypse:

If the State cannot survive the anti-slavery agitation, then let the State perish. If the Church must be cast down . . . then let the Church fall, and its fragments be scattered to the four winds of heaven, never more to curse the earth. If the American Union cannot be maintained . . . then let the American Union be consumed by a living thunderbolt, and no tear be shed over its ashes. If the Republic must be blotted out from the roll of nations . . . then let the Republic sink between the waves of oblivion, and a shout of joy, louder than the voice of many waters, fill the universe at its extinction.

Mr. Baldwin claimed only that:

In order to survive as a human, moving, moral weight in the world America and all the Western nations will be forced to . . . discard nearly all the assumptions that have been used to justify their lives and their anguish and their crimes so long.

But he did invoke Biblical furies—the threat to Noah—in the slave song of his peroration (". . . no more water, the fire next time").*

And his audience was overwhelmed. Long before the "Letter" appeared in book form it had been hailed in reviews for its clarity and understanding. Essays were written in description of the sensations of readers who pursued the piece through the columns of the *New Yorker,* now receiving revelation, now being distracted by a perfume ad

---

* Lately the other regions of Mr. Baldwin's mind seem, as may be noted, similar in terrain. A sympathetically treated character in this writer's novel *Another Country* remarks: "Some days, honey, I wish I could turn myself into one big fist and grind this miserable country [America] into powder. Some days I don't believe it has the right to exist."

—and clerics (the Bishop of the Episcopal Diocese of Western Massachusetts, for one example) used the "Letter" as the text of Lenten Messages. An occasional writer paused in his praise to mention "politics." Mr. Norman Podhoretz, who placed Mr. Baldwin's essay "among the classics of our language," observed in *Commentary* that the "tragic fact is that love is not the answer to hate—not in the world of politics, at any rate." But this remark appeared in an article ("My Negro Problem—And Ours") which itself attempted to "personalize" the entire matter of race relations. The author began with autobiography, re-creating the "twisted feelings" he had experienced as child and adult in his relations with Negroes. And he concluded with an assertion that miscegenation itself was the only reasonable answer to the problem:

The Black Muslims, like their racist counterparts in the white world, accuse the "so-called Negro leaders" of secretly pursuing miscegenation as a goal. The racists are wrong, but I wish they were right, for I believe that the wholesale merging of the two races is the most desirable alternative for everyone concerned. I am not claiming that this alternative can be pursued programmatically or that it is immediately feasible as a solution; obviously there are even greater barriers to its achievement than to the achievement of integration. What I am saying, however, is that in my opinion the Negro problem can be solved in this country in no other way.

Mr. Baldwin's other enthusiasts did not take this last step. But with only one important exception—F. W. Dupee, whose shrewd comments on the book appeared as the leading article of the first issue of the *New York Review* —they were certain that *The Fire Next Time* was a pinnacle of illumination. And implicit in that assessment was yet another explanation of the apathy and boredom that greeted press releases about young Negro college students arriving in Harlem to work as institutional aides.

"The longer I live," said Péguy, "the less I believe in the efficiency of an extraordinary sudden social revolution, improvised, marvelous, with or without guns and impersonal dictatorship, and the more I believe in the efficiency of modest, slow, molecular, definitive, social work." Pleasing in pace and movement, these words can't finally be invoked without uneasiness here. To stand firm for modest, uncharged, institutional modes of "social work" is not only to forgo "audience appeal," as the epigraph announces, it is to appear to minimize torment. Reason isn't speechless in the face of those who mock a century of "tokenism"; it can cite evidence that Negroes have only in recent decades committed themselves to the struggle for freedom, or it can instance the opinion of the archetypal objective observer, Gunnar Myrdal, who regards the advances of the last twenty years as phenomenal. But for the wounded such citations are poor balm. The student who sat in and lost an eye for his pains, the men and women who walked for months to "earn the right" to ride where they pleased, the newspaper editors and professors hounded from their jobs for refusing to cant, the Negro county agent who, in Ralph McGill's heart-shaking story, renovated the interior of his house but left the exterior a shambles "to avoid trouble," Miss Lucy, Mr. Meredith, Mr. Gantt, children mauled or murdered, parents who, waiting in cars at school, peer suddenly into a chaos of glassen splinters, blood, screeching forms— these deserve a voice commensurate to the claims of agony, not merely to the claims of order. From Martin Luther King they hear the demand for justice:

When a contemporary President declares . . . that all the massive resources of the Federal Government will enforce every constitutional right of Negroes he will split the reluctant and resisting South in two. . . . Their opposition will crumble before an implacable government, the desegregation across the South could be achieved in less than a year. The key to everything is Federal commitment, full, unequivocal, and unremitting.

From the Department of Justice they hear a U.S. deputy attorney general, Mr. Nicholas deB. Katzenbach, developing the mystique of tension:

The measure of a civilization . . . is the degree to which its citizens voluntarily conform to otherwise unenforceable laws. Yet it is dangerous to press law too far. A community may embody its best standards, its ideals and aspirations, in the law and look to the influence of the law to pull its habits and institutions toward its goals. And there can and should be a tension, but if the tension grows too great, if the gulf between the law and the attitudes of the community becomes too wide, the spring may snap and put the whole rule of law in danger.

But amid this confusion the havoc cry of the man of the apocalypse is also in their ears, and of the three voices it is the last, the voice of Mr. Baldwin, that alone *makes pain matter*. Without the scream of fury, in short, pain conceivably would not know itself and the world of institutions would not encounter, often enough, the world of feeling.

But in the name of the odd dialectic of American progress the screamers must in their turn be talked up to, even at the risk of encouraging complacency and obliviousness. They must be faced with the general truth—Tocqueville was first to assert it—that intensifications of the rage for reform occur when change occurs, and testify not to new disasters but to a new access of belief in the possibility of change. And they need also to be faced with the concrete demands for recognition of citizens who, although unacquainted with the *Fantasia of the Unconscious* and perhaps unenamoured of death, have elected to serve justice with labor. Do these citizens constitute a great host? Hardly. Bus riders and sit-ins and a few thousand school children; people who go door to door (encountering minor crudities and embarrassments) seeking signers for petitions that will commit their communities against discriminatory housing; college students to the number of one hundred and seventy-five who spend a summer teaching hard subjects to Negro school children . . . Dennis Westbrooks, aged 24, at the Kennedy Memorial Center in Harlem, who assists a group worker "in developing vocational guidance-teenage programs, and attempts to 'raise horizons' " . . . Kelton Sams, aged 19, at the Abraham Lincoln Community Center, who assists a group worker "in developing a leadership training program" . . . Roy Devoe, aged 31, at the Interdepartmental Neighborhood Services Center, who "concentrates on a neighborhood and family approach to delinquency" . . . Possessed of no rhetoric, troubled (many of them) by their unprotected commitment to decency, these figures come quickly to perceive that at the gritty bottom of some resistance to change lies—not hatred but ordinary human laziness and self-absorption. The perception is neither exhilarating nor depressing. Nothing better can be said for it—this piece of reality, experience as found—than that it constitutes the frail underpinnings of faith in "the efficiency of modest, slow, molecular, definitive, social work." And those who shrug off that faith while crying up cataclysm have proved, to repeat, that they also serve. But they do not serve themselves—here is the ineluctable which lightens regret, finally, about the response to the project on West 137th Street. In creating the abstract dream of unconditioned freedom Apocalyptic Man shakes the world, but loses touch with it, loses touch with the sense of others, the awareness of general life. And it remains a fact that this sense is all that stands between many men, here or in "other countries," and the fire *this* time: the furnace of absolute self-love or absolute self-contempt.

1963

Oyiemu-O?

All at once, seemingly, to homeland hisses and Anglo-Saxon applause, the "native novelists" of the world were telling tales in English: was it safe to trust their words?

A no answer to the question was a fool's answer, according to bookish opinion. And viewed in an apolitical context, the opinion was thoroughly understandable. No doubt the *Times Literary Supplement* sounded a bit blimpish in dismissing West African and Indian complaints that the novelists of these areas are "misrepresenting the native experience" (the paper attacked the complainants for failing to grasp that novels are "partial and cannot avoid giving offense"). And no doubt sensible readers would bear in mind the temptation to exotica facing writers of little-known lands who produce books mainly for export. But among literary folk neither concession amounted to much. What counted was that, time and again in the past, novelists slated in mid-career as exoticizers or falsifiers have ended by establishing themselves as seers. And, for minds trained to respect the past, the act of shrugging off these instances (approving the complaints against "native writers" appeared to require nothing less) constituted a near breach of professional codes.

That the reluctance to commit such a breach was understandable, though, did not in itself prove it was wise. Imaginative writers found wanting at home because they dare to represent their countrymen unfavorably are easy to defend: simply invoke the title Satirist and recall previous episodes of outrage among the satirized. But the situation is otherwise when writers are found wanting, say, for their sympathy with tragic views of history. And, as it happens, the misgivings stirred by the native novelists of the present are in fact traceable in some measure to their tragic rather than to their satiric themes. The item that molds these themes, moreover—a theory of history linking the fall of man with the advent of civilization, and rehabilitating the metaphor of the noble savage—is one that civilized people themselves do not always treat with favor. The truth is, to speak flatly, that reservations about the fictional voice of the new nations are not mere signs of local exacerbation at comic pictures of black men. They are, instead, part of a developing argument about the nature and meaning of the civilization into which those nations—people by the hundreds of millions—are now entering. And implicit in them is a critical problem, that

of the relation between art and social aspiration, which
no amount of muttering about oversensitive or naïve
audiences can possibly wish away.

As should be said, the summary of the new novelists'
themes as "tragic" needs to be qualified. The African folk
tales of Amos Tutuola ask to be thought of as a long
lament for a fabulous past—but the fabulous hero and
heroine of *The Palm-Wine Drunkard* and *The Brave
African Huntress* can't be called doleful types. The novelists of Trinidad who tell of their countrymen's London
experience of civilization focus on *anomie* as a condition
of whites and blacks alike ("Under the kiff-kiff laughter,"
says the narrator of Samuel Selvon's *The Lonely Lon-
doners,* "a great aimlessness, a great restless, swaying
movement . . . a kind of misery and pathos and a
frightening—What?")—but their books are often very
funny indeed. R. K. Narayan permits Indian characters to
dwell on the directionlessness of "high" civilization (" 'The
whole of the West is in a muddle owing to its political
consciousness,' " says Gajapathy in *The English Teacher,*
"and what a pity that the East should follow suit")—but
Narayan is one of the few writers alive who have advanced to the other side of tragedy, and none of his books
serves a simple argument. It is the work of younger writers,
significantly, that justifies a description of the native
novelist as a man enraptured by the past and distressed by
the present. And for some of the books in question reactionary seems, initially at least, a perfectly sensible label.

Consider, for example, the work of Chinua Achebe,
the thirty-year-old Nigerian author of *Things Fall Apart*
(1959) and *No Longer At Ease* (1961). Stories of fathers

and sons, Achebe's novels are attempts to render the inward experience of Nigerian generations that have simultaneously inhabited two worlds. Okonkwo *père,* the hero of *Things Fall Apart,* is an ambitious and masterful member of a primitive culture rich in feasts, battles, oracles, scapegoats, bad weather, and black passions—but from the start (the late nineteenth century) he is conscious of the coming of white emissaries of new religion and unassailable power, and in the end this power destroys him. Okonkwo *fils,* the hero of *No Longer At Ease,* is an ambitious member of a contemporary, graft-ridden, Lagos bureaucracy rich in Cokes and cocktails, nylons and whitewalls—but from the start he is engaged in an effort to cope with tribal as well as with bureaucratic idols, and in the end this effort destroys him. The likeness of the fates is suggestive, but the novelist is concerned less with continuities than with discontinuities. He portrays the old world as relatively un-self-conscious and the new as sick with self. His tribal generation is in constant encounter with two kinds of energy, clarity, and rigor—that of the poised commanding colonial, that of the vibrant, iron-browed chieftain; while his bureaucratic generation, exposed to whining tribesmen and embarrassed colonial lame ducks who are "fascinated" with the black man's looks and manners, knows only fatuity and confusion. And these differences determine the shape of his tales. The younger Okonkwo in *No Longer At Ease* is an introspective university graduate who hopes to elevate ethical standards among public servants; in telling of the ruin of his hopes, and of his decline into graft, the novelist seems bent upon showing him forth as a victim of a general cultural situa-

tion, rather than as a figure of personal weakness. At one
stage in the descent young Okonkwo hears a group of
traders singing a familiar song:

> An in-law went to see his in-law
> Oyiemu-o
> His in-law seized him and killed him
> Oyiemu-o
> Bring a canoe, bring a paddle
> Oyiemu-o
> The paddle speaks English
> Oyiemu-o

Laboring hard to translate the refrain into English, he
comprehends at length that it is a comment on two great
"betrayals"—the murder of an in-law ("a man's in-law was
his *chi,* his personal god"), and the snapping of the bond
of language that united the tribe: the "burden of the
song was 'the world turned upside down.'" Insofar as it
crystallizes incertitude, ambivalence, and probing doubt,
the translated tag stands as a key passage for both of
Achebe's novels.

The books described possess more than sociological
interest. They are strong in observation, and there is
authority in an account of a young bureaucrat's guilt at
accepting tribal scholarships for legal studies (his tribe
considered itself to be in need of trustworthy legal service),
and thereafter dropping those studies to read English
literature. (Achebe began his higher education meaning
to become a doctor; after winning scholarships at a government secondary school and later at the medical school

of the University College, Ibadan, he shifted to the liberal arts.) The author is likably proud of his literariness: he finds his titles in Yeats and Eliot, is preoccupied with centers that don't hold, doesn't scold his hero for taking pleasure in overheard remarks reminiscent of some accent of "Gerontion" or "Prufrock," and is in many respects the best-disciplined writer-in-English that his country has produced. (Aside from Tutuola the other Nigerian novelists of note are Cyprian Ekwensi, T. M. Aluko, and Onuora Nzekwu.) But as yet his talent deserves regard as a symptom rather than as an independent force. Its responsiveness to the modern literary voices of reaction and its disposition to set up contrasts between the organic coherence of the remote past and the discontinuities of the present bespeak attitudes toward the "revolution of rising expectations" that are considerably less exuberant than the phrase itself. And the appearance of similar attitudes in novelists even younger than Achebe (the youngest is Nzekwu, whose *Wand of Noble Wood,* a first novel, was published in London last year) suggest that they are likely to be dominant for some time.

Assessing the adequacy or appropriateness of these attitudes is no comfortable task. Current literary sophistication, as everyone knows, is hostile to the practice of testing fictional visions against objective reports. And it would seem in any event that, given the language barrier, such a practice would be impossible even if sophistication were persuaded to sanction it. The celebrated language barrier, however, is not everywhere as imposing as it was in former days. A number of nations, determined to unify territories divided by tribal dialects, are themselves encouraging the use of English. (Some have welcomed foreign pedagogical assistance: U.S. Government enterprises in English-teaching abroad range from Peace Corps projects to fellowship programs of AID.) And a good many sub-literary "organs of communication" have already adopted the new tongue. Reporters and editors from Fruta to Surabaja, Kumasi to Benghazi, journals of parrot isles and golden valleys, the Zanzibar *Voice* and the Kingston *Gleaner,* the Basutoland *News* and the Penang *Echo,* the *Billboard* of Belize and the *Post* of Bangkok, the *Pioneer* of Ashanti and the Port-au-Prince *Sun*—all are now telling time in English. As guides to the quality of experience in the lands they serve, such publications have clear limitations—which is simply to say again that they are far from offering fixed standards for the "evaluation" of imaginative writers. But they do offer the monolingual shut-in further glimpses of two characters—the lame-duck colonial and the awakened native—who often occupy the center of the novelists' canvas. And, interestingly, this supplementary evidence works to validate the imaginary portraits.

To say this isn't to claim—about the voice of the colonial, for instance—that nowhere in the world does it speak with the air of imperturbable rectitude familiar to Okonkwo *père* and others of the vanishing generation in Africa. An occasional newspaper account of a confrontation of magistrate and prisoner tells between its lines of the survival of the assumption that the distance between white and black is akin to that between man and beast— witness the following recent report of a trial:

Thuhloana Sephelka, elder of the Round Dance Church of Mottokoa's Village, appeared at the Teyateyaneng Magistrate's Court before Mr. R. S. Balfe on a charge of culpable homicide.

Ma-Saetsang Sephelka, the wife of the accused, in her evidence said that on the 7th January of [1962] she went to see the headman's wife after sunset. On her return her husband hit her. He then took a stick intending to hit her on the head. She turned her head and the three month old baby received the blow on the head.

The following morning she noticed that the baby's head was swollen and took it to the medical officer. The baby died a few minutes after it had been examined. A post mortem examination revealed that death was due to a fractured skull and brain haemorrhage.

Summing up, Mr. Balfe reproached the habit of the Basuto of striking their assailants on the heads with sticks. [Sephelka] was found guilty and sentenced to 18 months imprisonment with hard labor.

But the unastonished correspondent and magistrate—men whose impersonal assurance provided older generations with a clarifying object of hatred—appear regularly only in the South African press (the item quoted is from the Basutoland *News*). Throughout most of the underdeveloped world the reported character of the colonial lame duck is marked by fussiness and absurdity rather than detachment and will. From a Rhodesian news service comes word that the country's National Resources Board, headed by a Mr. P. Deedes, "is launching an appeal to cover the cost of reintroducing White Rhinoceros to Southern Rhodesia." The *Daily Gleaner* of Kingston fills its letter columns in midsummer with complaints against a radio interviewer who, reporting a royal visit, "kept referring to Her Royal Highness, Princess Margaret, as 'she' . . ." The Central African *Post* teases itself with hopes of a British defection from the UN. (Reporting a London dinner meeting of the Nyasaland Club, the paper takes pugnacious satisfaction in a disingenuous remark of R. A. Butler's to the effect that he "wonder[ed] what Rhodes would have thought of the United Nations.") Even the sentimentality of the Tory Romantic as tourist is losing its purity. An Englishman writing on the primitive fishermen of the Costa da Caparica begins with a paean to men who sweat for their bread (" 'When Adam delved/ And Eve span' they did so at 'subsistence level' and probably the fisheries of the Sea of Galilee provided for daily wants and little more"), but after a moment he slips out of romance into cold-war pragmatics:

Entirely out of date, uneconomic, what you will, but these shipbuilders and those tartan-clad, stocking-capped fishermen . . . represent a valuable reserve of ancient craftsmanship. In these days of progress when civilization may be wiped out from one day to another by ultra-modern nuclear engines of destruction, these old boys may still be very useful. It is well to keep candles in the house against a power breakdown. [*Anglo-Portuguese News*]

And the pervasive note on the Dark Continent—sometimes amusing, sometimes tearful, rarely so much as dogged—is that of farewell and dissolution. "Owing to termination of partnership," says the classified advertisement in the Bulawayo *Chronicle,* "tenders are invited for the purchase of a gold mine." "Mr. Smart of the Nairobi [Kenya] City Council," reports the Central Africa News Service, "sadly appeals to quitting settlers to send any . . . material which could be useful for compiling a history of Nairobi's early years to the Nairobi Mayor's Parlour." Things fall apart.

As for the experience of the new educated classes and bureaucrats: here again the non-literary evidence argues strongly for the reasonableness of the fictional view. According to that view, as found in both Indian and Nigerian novels, educated youth in the underdeveloped nations knows two kinds of torment—the insistent Western hard sell which equates virtue with buying power and stimulates impossible desires, and the insistent inward fear that new corruption, old superstition, and expanding mass media are preparing a path for charismatic (or fascist) leaders. The hard-selling ad, a staple of the newspaper-in-English abroad, sings of a thousand "needs"—from Ovaltine to Morris Minors, roundworm expellers to fountain pens. But regardless of the nature of the object hawked, the act of purchase is defined invariably as a step toward self-realization. (A typical, widely placed ad carries the head-line HIGH STANDARDS above a photograph of two Negroes, one impressionable and eager-eyed, the other white-coated, supervisory; the text reads as follows:

The skilled young worker takes careful note of the manager's instruction. Soon he will be promoted because the manager has noted the high standard of his work. The manager has also noted with approval the young man's Parker Pen. For Parker pens are made to the highest standard in the world.

That is why the manager himself chose a Parker, as you can see by the famous . . . clip in his pocket. If you are a young man of energy and ambition, the superb Parker '17' is the pen for you. . . . IF YOU ARE AMBITIOUS YOU WILL WANT A PARKER PEN.

The second torment, anguish about the entanglements of corruption and charisma, is obviously genuine in present-day Nigeria. According to the London *Observer,* the government of that nation has for months been conducting an investigation of the public corporations of the Western Region (the latter control millions of pounds), with the aim of finding sufficient evidence of corruption to launch a movement against the area's independently powerful chief. (The probe has given rise thus far not only to charges and countercharges, but to insurrectionary plotting and repressive police action.) What is more, among the new states there are several—Ghana, for one—where the language of the press itself testifies to the justice of concern about manipulated superstition. Ghanian newspapers are all miracle and melodrama—and the Threatening Enemy is, naturally, the robber bureaucrat-politico. Nkrumah the Good survives the "wicked bomb attacks" of "grafters" and "scoundrels" because the Lord respects him, and it is as the interpreter of this special relation that the press plays its political role. News columns tell in plain style of "escape celebrations" held in honor of Osagyefo the President—mass dancing of the "ewe dance" to the music of "borborbar." Faithfully they detail the presentation of gifts to the Leader (a cow, a dozen pigeons, some kola), and the performance of high rituals (the speaker of the National Assembly drapes Osagyefo in white cloth to signify his victory over his enemies, others anoint him with the blood of a white sheep offered for sacrifice, and Madam Josephine Ehaonond-Blay pours lavender over his feet). But the editorial pages, more venturesome, announce that BOMB SPOT SHALL BE A SACRED SHRINE, and explain that:

. . . in just over five minutes after the explosion a torrential rainfall [came] answering the fury of violent storms and lightning. On this same day of the bomb atrocity . . . there was an eclipse of the sun in Ghana. . . . Long live the Leader, Master, Teacher, Founder, Father, Inspirer, the Torch, the Pilot, the Guide, the Fountain of Honour, Our Osagyefo the Messiah . . .

And on the women's page of the same paper (the Ghana *Times*), below a headline reading NO SOFT DEAL WITH THE EVIL TRIO, and adjacent to comic strips (Flash Gordon, the Lone Ranger) and astrologists, a forthright woman's columnist named Nancy Chochoe Plange fills her space as follows:

Just imagine the situation our country would have been ditched in if these 'despicable rats' (with apologies to traitor Adamafio) had succeeded in their evil intentions. Oh God, thou art good and wonderful. . . . The nation will never accept a soft deal with these rogues. We also believe that they were not alone in their evil machinations; let's comb the nation well and bring their accomplices to book, those silly selfish ne'er-do-wells who want to lie in soft-padded beds while honey drips into their hellish mouths. Damn them! To hell with them!

Darting erratically from century to century, Miss Chochoe
Plange's diction ("thou art" as against "soft deal," "evil
machinations" as against "to hell with them") provides a
tonal microcosm of temporal discontinuity—and thus, in
addition, an analogue of a sort for the wild cab drivers of
Lagos whose custom (says Mr. Achebe) is to seek out dogs
to run over in order to "bring good luck for car." But the
prime interest of her column is as a reminder that in the
new nations fear of the perversion of literacy isn't idle.

To repeat: accepting a basket of clippings as a satisfactory substitute for methodologically sound research is
risky; the case for "reaction" cannot be tried in the newspapers. But there are other, relevant, and less disreputable
repositories of evidence. Professionally skilled inquirers
into the transformation of the underdeveloped world often
draw attention to chaos and cruelty as concomitants of
the change. A few years ago, discussing the experience of
urban workers in the new nations, Eugene Black remarked
(in his *Diplomacy of Economic Development*) that these
people are "plunged into a bewildering, formless, insecure
life, requiring a whole new set of attitudes. . . ." The tale
of the Chinese "forward leap," even when set forth by
as unhysterical an observer as Edgar Snow, remains one of
appalling human sacrifice. The most powerful sections of
Robert Heilbroner's book on the underdeveloped world,
The Great Ascent, are concerned to demonstrate that the
dynamics of the "development revolution" are those of
human dislocation. ("The great social transformation of
development," writes this economist, "is apt to be marked
not by rising expectations but by a loss of traditional expectations, not by enjoyable gains but by a new awareness

of deprivation.") And books have already been written on the precise nature of the psychological strains of transformation (the most interesting of them is Everett Hagan's treatise *On the Theory of Social Change*).

What can be said, in sum, is that neither the untendentious reports of outsiders nor the highly tendentious pages of the "local" press provide much justification for a dismissal of the novelistic version of experience in the underdeveloped nations. If the clarities of the lost world now being rediscovered and re-evaluated were harsh, they were nonetheless clarities. If the emergent "mixed attitudes" toward the revolution are surprising at first glance, they become less so on scrutiny. And if these attitudes are rejected abruptly as products of self-indulgent fantasy or nostalgic exoticism, the rejection must be made in the name not of fact but of faith.

From all this it doesn't follow, of course, that the faith in question is narrow or mean. The freshly admired world of coherence and value is also, as the novelists' critics are aware, the world in which an Iranian peasant goes blind because he cannot find the three dollars and ninety-four cents that he believes he must have in order to be treated, in which bludgeoned infants bleed to death untended, and in which a billion human beings "enjoy a standard of living 'less than $100 a year.' " (The statistic is provided in Mr. Heilbroner's volume, which includes a moving report on what families can and cannot do, round the world, on less than one hundred dollars a year.) And there is meaning in disease and hunger and violence as well as in "values." To be sure, the imagination doesn't suffer by the numbers. And the universal fashionableness of irony makes it difficult for any writer to offer a joyful vision of young minds awakening into the world of created beauty —the world not simply of books but of individual aspiration. And the elementary political fact remains that the "great ascent" to a decent standard of living probably cannot be managed under democratic forms. But still the snag catches. Extraordinary possibilities have been glimpsed; an end to a thousand torments has been envisaged: is it inconceivable that a thoughtful and generous mind might, in the contemplation of a prospect once literally unimaginable, find itself compelled to exuberance, boomed (as it were) into buoyancy? Is not this literary finickiness about Progress one more proof of the justice of the famous promulgation about the two cultures—the gospel that ticked off the humanist as inhuman?

The traditional answer to such questions, namely that the voice of the imaginative writer was the original voice of freedom, lacks force. The day of English sonnets on the cause of freedom in Haiti is past: there has been no literary language for the expression of generalized aspiration, social or political, for many years.* And criticism currently doubts that such a language can ever exist again —as this comment by Auden makes clear:

* The new novelist of an underdeveloped nation who attempts to find such a language strikes most experienced readers as crude. Cyprian Ekwensi of Nigeria describes his first book, *People of the City* (1954), as an attempt to dramatize his hero's "genuine determination to be part of the rapidly growing, political, social, and cultural development of his country." An English critic, Martin Banham, writing in a recent issue of the *Review of English Literature,* speaks of Ekwensi as "a good journalist but non-creative. . . ."

The relation of a poet, or any artist, to society and politics is, except in Africa or still backward semifeudal countries [the exception need not be made any longer], more difficult than it has ever been because, while he cannot but approve of the importance of everybody getting enough food to eat and enough leisure, this problem has nothing whatever to do with art, which is concerned with *singular persons,* as they are alone and as they are in their personal relations. Since these interests are not the predominant ones in his society; indeed in so far as it thinks about them at all, it is with suspicion and latent hostility—it secretly or openly thinks that the claim that one is a singular person, or a demand for privacy, is putting on airs, a claim to be superior to other folk—every artist feels himself at odds with modern civilization.

Neither is it helpful to answer meachingly that, since the literary voice is at present only one among dozens of competing voices, its crotchetiness, irrelevance, or inadequacy "does no harm": the step from here to a total discount of imaginative literature is too short.

The one reasonable retort is that the reactionary gestures of the new literatures-in-English are at bottom gestures of consciousness—and therefore must be understood as notification first of all of an ascent achieved, not of an ascent despised. The point is complicated; it doesn't appear on maps that show the world as an assemblage of opposites—leftists vs. rightists, sickness vs. health, and the like; its weight can be felt only if the truism that civilization equals consciousness is held firmly in mind. But it does have weight. The principle of growth in a society is the principle of innovation, and, as Everett Hagan remarks in his analysis of social change, "any acceptance of a cultural trait from outside is innovation; there is no such thing as passive imitation." In planning their economic development on Western models, the new nations open themselves to technical sophistication. In imitating Western models of social criticism, in defining the threat of dislocation implicit in the "development revolution," the new novelists open their world to sophistication about culture itself. Their voices announce the advent of minds that occupy a world of choices, that have had intuitions of multiplicity, that grasp the limitations of wholism and understand the usefulness of attempts to body forth the reality of parts.

The telescoping of historical process involved in these attempts is, admittedly, jarring. That nations struggling for release from "natural simplicity"—in the form of the wild drum and bludgeon—should produce pastoralists; that writers whose countrymen turn eyes of longing toward the West should respond by invoking English poets on the sickness of the West; that men of sensibility can blot from sight clinics, nurses, schools, scholarships, the whole apparatus of Progress, and listen instead with inward ear to the song of *oyiemu-o,* the world turned upside down—all this is extraordinary. The likelier event would have been for writers to turn themselves into servants of the dogmas of production. But in the West the artist is the critic of dogmas—those of depression as well as of euphoria. And the decision of the novelists of the emerging countries to follow the Western model, instead of the model of the artist as party hack, may in the end be no occasion for international tears.

For if any report can be trusted, critics of dogmas are

needed in these nations. To speak against the public definition of the good when that definition is deprecated by
everyone capable of thought is, true enough, to be a
cliché-monger (the Western literary world is over-popu-
lated with the latter). But to speak as a critic of the
public definition of the good when that definition stands
unquestioned, when aspiration and overexpectation seem
universal, when in the Lagos streets bicycling youngsters
wear placards on their backs announcing all confidently
FUTURE MINISTER—this is at once to meet a public need
and to function as a civilized man.

No doubt there are dangers in satisfying such needs—
more of them than are apparent to oblivious literary minds
that see every issue in terms of the old wars of artists and
philistines. The young novelist of Nigeria enthralled with
Eliot's lines about the magi—

> We returned to our places, these Kingdoms,
> But no longer at ease here, in the old dispensation,
> With an alien people clutching their gods

—may well persuade many that the new alienation is
worse than the old dispensation. But it is at least as likely
that he will help to establish awareness that human problems survive social transformation, and thereby ease the
enormous and inevitable disappointments which, in other
overexpectant worlds, have led to violent reactionary rage.
By protesting in the name of *his* feelings, he lays it force-
fully down that the "revolution of rising expectations" is a
billion revolutions, numberless contradictory wellings of
perversity, passion, industry, and sloth which, because inward and personal, cannot ever be fully comprehended in

the flat public language of success or failure. And to possess this knowledge is to possess precisely that human consciousness, clear, complex, unillusioned, which is the ideal destination of the ascent.

1963

Glossing a
Portuguese
Diary

Entry for a wet winter evening, the end of a stay at a port
quinta *on the Douro River in the north country:*

—The Colonel's nephew, N., came into view tonight, and the result was a moment. Could it have been predicted? Perhaps not by an American. N. is Oxbridge, thirty-two, unmarried; third man once in a no-capital London publishing house now defunct, subscriber to the *New Statesman, Spectator,* and the old *Universities and Left*—great unread mounds of the first two in a litter on the floor at one side of his bedroom desk—and owner of a red Austin Sprite, a Webcor tape recorder, and a store of used tapes (a "library" of Portuguese song, dance, "interviews": symbols of the old and the true, the pure European past). He came out several years ago from

England after an operation, intending to spend a warm
October; at the moment he has no plans for returning.
When he spoke the first night he sounded unlike the usual
thoughtful traveller, the character who claims to be fascinated with Portugal and in fact only sees the place
through books. In diffident voice with touches of irony,
after the ladies had left and while the Colonel gently
snored over his glass, he explained the country—as follows:

"The old man" (Salazar) believes that the modern world
can be bled a bit, enough to support a revitalization of
Portuguese tradition. "The old man" believed this thirty
years ago and believes it still and (despite the Angolan
crisis) may well have a successor who agrees with him.
For the country to exist it needs a certain amount of
foreign coin, hence it slicks out main roads and their
environs, certain cities and towns, tourist areas—Estoril
of course and the whole Costa do Sol—in a way that wins
friends and justifies the adjective in the favorite p. r.
phrase: Portugal, the New State. The country also needs
to expand its industrial plant, if it is to put an end to
money crises—hence it worries about transportation,
harries its businessmen about inefficiency, improves the
education of some of the populace, and proceeds (slowly)
with a public-health program. But newness isn't really
desired at all: the object is to achieve what is necessary
for survival without accepting any "fundamentally indigestible" element of modern civilization. A strong
Church, a Responsible Aristocracy, a Protected Womanhood, and a Guild System—these are the ideals, while
Admass and illiterate literacy and consumers' madness

and faceless labor organization (N. did not use the word America in this speech) are the enemies.

Who let in Lady Docker, the tabloid heroine? N. shrugged at this and grinned when mention was made of his fleet Sprite and the splendid indigestible nickelodeons assembled by an English firm in Spain) that belt out rock and roll at Estoril and Praia da Rocha, and certainly the subject seemed to die naturally. And during the wilderness excursions of the last days—Trás-os-Montes, rambles through great stone fields gaping at nature's Henry Moores, pauses in remote villages, an hour spent watching village dancers perform "as they did five hundred years ago"— the party came together at moments (again: as it seemed) in a decent consciousness of guilt. Even at today's picnic, eaten in a drizzle in a ruined Cistercian monastery under the eyes (was it only for the last five minutes?) of a peasant mother and child. A lavish meal as always—pink gins, three kinds of *pâté,* turkey, beef, sweetbreads, port, brandy, taken with much hilarity until the audience came. The audience stood in an archway: the mother a dirty, stately woman with a swaddled baby in her arms—"They won't give *up* swaddling"—and a daughter, say, five years old, at her side. Keeping out of the rain, watching patiently, uttering no word, none of the hissing *pobre, pobre* of the trained *mendigo* back home. The Colonel's chauffeur was dispatched with a bagful of leavings, picked bones, gnawed slabs of bread, pits and tins; he handed it to the child as the mother unsmiling half curtsied (N. answered by touching his hat brim), and the child peeked in at the contents. Her expression—shy glee, mistrust, wonder—stopped the throat. She darted away, the mother curtsied again, and thereafter: an awkward silence. The impression then was that seemly self-laceration was in process, and perhaps for an instant a memory of some item of his past, "leftism and all that," did trouble N. But to judge from tonight's stories, the main effect of the occasion was to clarify a vision.

"A fine place for a vision"—this could be (will be) written in the guest book without a trace of hypocrisy. The low-ceilinged, bare-beamed, white dining room upstairs floated in a sea of heavy odors—duck, orange, flaming brandy, port, Jermyn Street cigars. Rain beating along the shutters on the river side, monster *serra* dogs grumbling on the hearth, aching for a Heathcliffian boot, the Colonel dozing (bobbing and weaving), N. hidden in smoke. Levitation proceeded. N. had not been in the country long, he said ruminatively, when he'd naturally felt compelled to go to Porto in search of a girl: how was he to explain why he had found not a common slut but a creature whose interest in him was utterly personal, warm, open—absolutely determined to put money out of consideration? Hard to answer though not disquieting—but what would come next? N. poured and resumed. He was not sentimental, he argued, but he could remember—here the Colonel grunted awake and the dogs growled and the fire cracked loudly and the candles guttered and the wind thomped—did the Colonel remember the night when Merido and [a Debretted eminence from England] were here in this room? Something extraordinary that night, a ripple of ancient feeling had gone round the room that night—unforgettable. The eminence and his lady were opening a library in ———; they'd come over for the weekend and the Colonel had invited his old steward to be of the party for a meal. Merido, the steward, had served the Colonel and his father faithfully, had profited at the first war by selling some timbered acreage at just the proper moment, on the Colonel's father's advice, and then had gone on to become a modest landholder. As they came to the table the old steward—grizzly fellow of great dignity and poise though moist-eyed—spoke for the first time, saying he was pleased that his excellency found it agreeable that a former carpenter and son of a carpenter be invited to sit at table with him. The eminence raised his eyebrows, offered a place deferentially with his hand, then smilingly reminded the old man that in history there had indeed been carpenters with whom official fools refused to break bread, and would anyone call them blessed? A beautiful speech, said N. generously, voice rising a little, a quality to the situation that belonged to another age despite all incongruities. Something there you couldn't see as Tories and Labour, hear hear, said the Colonel pouring; the dogs rose loudly and stretched and sighed. Whereupon the noise of the rain or a look of embarrassed puzzlement that he caught whipped N. on to a summit. "Do y'know something else? Apropos your nickelodeons and whatever. They don't matter. They don't go *deep* is the truth. I remember the second time I was around your lot, Estoril, the Costa. I was coming back in the car via Sintra, starting my trip on the Estrada. Out came the sirens, godawful racketing, Warra-Warra!"—the dogs bounded up roaring, the Colonel bellowed affably at them—"it was the President coming by with his motorcycles and his old Cadillac. He uses a summer palace at Cascais, perhaps you know. I heard the noise and just in the moment I saw a peasant woman, somebody's cook I expect, coming up from the station. I'd gone in to the curb thinking the siren was the *bombeiros*—I happened to look at her as they came by and what do you think?" (Pausing embattled, holding the eye.)

"She knelt."

N. let his breath out, relaxing. "The sense of dignity, there's what it is," he said more kindly, holding a dog's head in a hammer lock against his chest, blowing at the smoke to see his audience. "You dignify yourself by respecting, honoring in that way. I can tell you—without that feeling, without knowing it you haven't got a politics, you haven't—" A shutter crashed finishing this, banishing nickelodeons, Cadillacs, prosperous whores from the air. "It's true," he nodded again, "she knelt—she knelt as though the Virgin Herself were passing. . . ."

The Colonial English thus presented to the mind make a man wince, months after he has left them, in sympathy for their wounds and lost hopes. But their fantasies, to use the rudest word, are more relevant than might be supposed. Relevant to what? To the official program of the country, first of all, as this can be made out from sights and sounds and printed words—Salazar's *Doctrine and Action* (1939, Faber), for example, and various interviews with him that have been published in France and elsewhere in the past two decades. Since the chosen rhetoric of the program is statistical (Salazar is an economist), the thing has about it, as a mere abstraction, a queer cast of modernity, and its details bespeak a powerful faith in rigorous planning and specification. Specify the proper level of education for each position in the state down to the level of private chauffeur, specify (for a public-housing project) which block is to be occupied by cab drivers, which block is to be occupied by post-men, specify when the local workmen's associations (Sindicatos) and Employers' Associations (Grémios) and Agricultural Syndicates (Casas do Povo)* are to be recognized, abolished, federated, refederated, incorporated, or reincorporated. But the planners do look backward—to the happy serf, the resident landlord, Woman in the Home; in using the idiom and technology of advanced socioeconomics their ultimate purpose is, just as the Englishman indicated, to shore up a closed and piously anti-modern society. Which means that when you speak glowingly of bended knees, you address yourself to Portuguese life in terms officially regarded as highly appropriate.

Nor would it be right to claim that these terms are everywhere and always inappropriate. Eyes unsharpened by a thousand nights in Soho still turn up evidence of their own that the manners of Portuguese simple folk belong to another age. Down from the hills come the vintage workers in a winding file, aware that two weeks of almost unutterably exhausting labor lie ahead: the lady

---

* Shortly after a new constitution was adopted in 1933 a Labor Statute was "passed" which created the first of these odd groups—paper guilds, as it were. There are now hundreds of them, all organized into Federations, and there is a note of toy cash register fun in their formation. (In the last few years sixty new Casas do Povo have been formed, which in turn have been organized into thirteen Federations.) The Federations are gathered under the rubric "Full Corporations" of which there are now eight, covering the various industries. The Corporations, government-managed of course, "police" the Federations, and also undertake certain benevolent roles, as for example the management of holiday centers for workers.

owner of the *quinta* goes out to welcome them; their
leader sweeps his cap to the ground saying, *Minha senhora,*
we would have a vintage every month for the pleasure of
working your lugares. At a nine-thirty sunset in Alcácer
the hugely rich proprietor of a ranch climbs out of
a Mercedes in a barnyard as a procession of black-
hatted, black-shawled, barefooted girls comes across the
meadow after the workday: seeing him they fall silent, he
lifts his hand, calls out to one by name, and all salute
and reply in low, slow, somber voices, apologetic for the
noise of their conversation, *Boa tarr-r-r-de:* he joshes another and sets them gratefully smiling. At a bullfight in
the Campo Pequeno in Lisbon, the country's most famous
entertainer, the *fado*ist Amalia Rodriguez, rises to make
her way out early and is stopped by an old fellow wearing
a threadbare suit and a stained goatee, a stranger to her
party; with no air of offense all pause in leisurely respectful interest as he takes her fingers to his lips and makes a
brief speech expressing (with an easy gesture) the esteem
felt for the singer by those behind him in the cheaper
seats. Major J. attached to the American advisory military group drives his tail-finned CD station wagon up to
his rented house in Carcavelos and before he sounds the
horn his gardener and the gardener's son have drawn back
the gates with grave punctilio, as for a royal progress. "I
serve the Queen of Spain," says a groom of the Countess
of Barcelona grandly, smiling at coronets sewn on a
stinking horse blanket in Estoril; we represent "pride of
service" is the unspoken word of the servingmaids of
Lady X who stand at drilled attention before a luncheon
sideboard in the oldest house in Lisbon. The flow of

courtesy soothes not only the local gods—the ducal Pal-
mellas, Marqueses de Sabugosa, Condes de Carnide, and
the rest—and a hundred displaced lords and ladies of the
Continent (they flock to the Costa and stay to echo the
words of the much-mocked Lady Docker, who told the
Telegraph, Oh yes she was coming here again and again,
people treat you the way one expects to be treated, now
yis they does), but the meanest tourist in a three-dollar
pensão as well.

For the obeisance or abasement implicit in such courtesy—and of course for foreign visionaries who cherish it
—the liberal has a ready contempt. On his view nothing
matters except that Portugal has "no freedom, no morality, no bread." The last phrase was made by General Delgado, who has often sought support on the Continent for
Portuguese insurgent groups, and it needs little amplifica-
tion.* There is cruel poverty behind nearly every working-
class door in the north and south, and UNESCO health
statistics give the lie to those who say that sunshine is
food. And as for the accusation "no freedom," it is borne
out by one or another "political" event every month. A
poorly planned attempt at revolution is put down—military men, workers, and priests jailed; Salazar appears on
television, coldly defining the range of criticism that can
be tolerated by the government; a few weeks pass and
then in Lisbon the Portuguese Civil Army ("private citizens available only in the event of a national emergency")
parades in green before silent crowds, displaying weapons
that include the never obsolete Chicago sub-machine gun.

* Delgado was shot to death in 1965; his body was found just over the
border, in Spain.

The visitor to Oporto is told that several factory workers have been released after two years of imprisonment (without a trial) on charges of having sought to organize a union. He returns to Lisbon and learns that three professors at the university have been jailed for having written and caused to circulate a pamphlet complaining against the government's refusal to allow an English socialist into the country. When this episode is nearly "forgotten," word comes that Aquilino Ribeiro, a novelist said to have been writing in a simple realistic vein about life in the north, is to be brought to bar on some spurious charge. At any moment, in any city, the foreign paper that had hitherto been available at the *tabacaria* fails to turn up, and the newsdealer answers inquiry with the word, *Censura;* local journals are rarely less than evasive in their reporting of domestic news; a major daily that displeases the Censor has its press run trucked off to the Campo Grande and burned. It is all in the well-known grain: a political reality that constantly rouses (in a small circle) fury and frustration impossible to sophisticate into something other than what it is: a pure response to the suppression of personal freedom.

But although the liberal who concentrates here, on the black reality of the poverty-ridden totalitarian state, is considerably easier to admire than a man keening for what we have lost, and although the Marxist analysis he could make of a dozen elements in the national situation could not fail to enlighten, the depressing truth remains that his language is only a little more adequate for the expression of the Portuguese circumstances of greatest interest than the jargon of *noblesse oblige.* To say this is of course meaningless without specifying the nature of the circumstances. And the latter is an unrewarding task, for the circumstances in question seem at first glance a mere matter of jokes and juxtapositions, clashes of old and new: insignificant items at best. Granted the clash mentioned; granted that certain sections of the country offer a distracting topographical comedy featuring endless cheap gags about Time; granted that on the Glamorous Estrada of the Costa Alfa-Romeos toot wildly passing donkey carts, French girls in winter Bikinis buy pastry from Portuguese women drowning in a thousand layers of black, and *kitsch* castles (baroque air-conditioned grotesquery put up in imitation of the Tower of Belém), and luxury hotels (in the International Style), and private houses (on the model of swell St. Augustine or Santa Barbara) are separated by brooks, fields, and gulches where women beat sheets on boards, oxen pull wooden plows and farm workers build family dwellings of cane and clay—granted all this, why should any of it count? With contrasts of the same sort littering every town from Baghdad to Mobile, why give them so much as a word?

Partly (to come at once to an answer) because their absurdity stands as a precise analogue for the contradictions of means and ends in official policy that were hinted at before. Knowing that its factories are inefficient, and believing that uninterested, careless workers are to blame, the government exhorts the latter in a thousand ways to lay by what Salazar himself speaks of as the national inferiority complex—the unmistakable darkness, the sense of hopelessness expressed in the national music. Whitewash your village buildings once a year! (The painting

program was not undertaken solely to impress foreign
tourists but to alter a psychological landscape.) Think
constantly on our possessions! (Public buildings are
adorned with huge maps of Europe which have an overlay
of Portuguese territories establishing that "Portugal" is in
point of area greater than Europe; the maps bear the
legend, "Portugal is no small country.") Hear no *fados!*
(Salazar has set himself firmly against this music on the
ground that it is narcotic in effect.) So much from the
voice of authority—but so much and a great deal more.
Be proud! demands the voice—but also: Know your place
and don't move from it! Be gay, full of hope!—but also:
Honor those above you, accept the iron order which
specifies your position, the thin range of your pleasures,
the proper intensity of your piety. While the contradiction
implicit in such instructions may bring to mind a comic
turn—Willie Howard on the soapbox finishing a grand
peroration, then darting out a finger at his single auditor
and shouting fiercely: "Form a circle!"—the joke is cru-
elly manipulative and issues in bewilderment too poignant
to draw a smile.*

* The poor are not alone in this experience of bewilderment. Ambitious
men, those who win a measure of economic power and place themselves in
position to satisfy the appetites stimulated by news from the Funhouse
abroad, seem nevertheless to be required to regard themselves simultaneously as heroes and villains. As matters stand, if a manufacturer drives himself hard, he may contribute to the necessary improvement of Portuguese
trade balances. But if in doing so he becomes what is called a success, he
only qualifies for a fresh share of the new national guilt. His wife clicks
about the Chiado on high heels, arranges canasta parties, enters the world—
while the official voice insists that the one proper place for her is at home.
(When Teddy Boy vandalism—Portugal has not bothered to invent a name
of its own for delinquents—broke out a while ago at Queluz and at Praia
das Macas, the Police Communiqué in the press blamed the trouble mainly
on the wives of rich businessmen who leave their children to domestics and
spend their days at cards while their husbands pursue their *negociatas*.)

For a traveler it is of course possible to step back from this bewilderment, to ignore it or to regard the discovery of some item that occasions it as a ground for self-congratulation. A hint of the latter policy is present in the *New Statesman* reports that touch now and then on the alteration of psychological landscape just mentioned: these seem to suggest that, since a keen eye never misses the skull beneath the skin, the squalor under the paint, the only lesson in such an alteration is that liberals see through all stunts and lies. But plainly such a treatment will not do. Whether or not the Portuguese is melancholy and dark, he is beyond question often hungry and sick, and when he is in this condition the stunt, the transformation of his landscape, the false claim that here the glossy radiance of nature is mirrored in the things of man, can only mock his weakness. In Spain there is a unity of anguish for the eye, the mind, the memory; the "sense manifold" contradicts nothing, combines and mingles with the truths of history in a way that permits the wounded Spaniard to *be* his landscape. Hundreds of political prisoners are rotting in Burgos in sight of the splendid cathedral, yet it is fair to say that the filth-strewn city is all one, and for this reason, because a thousand seams of wretchedness are allowed to show through, it becomes a fit image of the heart-shaking pride and humiliation of its citizenry. But the ruined Portuguese goes an alien's progress through

And at any moment this same voice is likely to hunt him down in his office with the complaint that his methods are alien, as they indeed in one sense are, to "our higher goals." (Deprecating "cut-throat practices"—meaning American-style hustle and ruthlessness—the Portuguese Secretary of State for Commerce has publicly charged that "the sharpest competition which a Portuguese businessman has to face, both at home and abroad, comes from other business firms in this country.")

most of his villages. Drive northward on the Coimbra road and you pass one dazzling town after another, every dooryard neatly bricked, no mud, jasmine afire in the air, public fountains gleaming, walls radiant, almond blossoms seeming almost to twinkle whiteness out of the washed crystalline sky, clouds of wildflowers, uncorrupted green fields—a unified picturesque, a landscape of Snow White and the Dwarfs that refuses the starving or the halt even the comfort of an image of their own despair.

But there are always the healthy, it is said—what good would such comfort be to them? The assumption of the question is that the national schizophrenia does not affect everyone, that there are people who experience no violent yoking of opposite impulses, feel no cross-time beating in their brains. A mistaken assumption, to judge from the number of characters whose lives, while seeming to establish the possibility of "successful transition," in point of fact stand for chaos itself. In Lisbon four years ago Snr. A., a man now in his late thirties who speaks and writes several languages with grace and works as the chief of the parts division of the largest sports-car dealer in Portugal, was asked by his employer to drive a car for the firm in a celebrated French race. The purpose of the entry was to secure local publicity for the firm, and the Lisbon papers cooperated enthusiastically for some weeks before the race, carrying on their front pages pictures of the firm's elegant showrooms, stories about the car, the driver, the nature of the contest. Unfortunately Snr. A. had an accident during the race which demolished the car and sent him to the hospital for three months. At the end of this period his employer made a payroll-deduction arrangement which returned Snr. A. to the serf's condition, by "enabling" him to reimburse the firm not only for the ruined car but also for the expense of his medical care. And for the past four years the man has been working off this burden, living in the city on less than fifty dollars a month; he wears an abstracted expression, occasionally lacerates himself ("I made a mistake"), and sees his employer as a just and honorable master. Again: in the town of Maniche, Izaura B., a domestic aged seventeen and a handsome girl, no longer works with her mother in the evenings learning how to spell out words in an old newspaper, rising from the vale of illiteracy (her mother has had two months of schooling); Izaura's master has given her an old phonograph and she spends her evenings in a white mud hut (since Maniche is on the much traveled road from Sintra to Estoril and hence is visible to tourists, the town has electricity) listening over and over again to an LP of *Wonderful Town*. The priest's opinion has not yet been given. Or again: slim schoolboys from the Colegio de . . . , forbidden the Cinema, used to gather at noon every day at the Tamariz beach to gaze at naked foreign women lying on the sands, but one of their number, a boy of good family, attacked a woman in her cabana, with the result that all are now restricted to the football field. The boy in question is said to have explained that as he passed he was certain the woman "signalled" to him (the lady in the case has "admitted" that she might have been letting down a shoulder strap preparing to take the sun at the moment the boy went by), and to have indicated that the official or unofficial word passed in the school is that the women of the Costa in bikinis are without exception French whores.

But the multiplication of examples—mere incongruities

and jokes—is pointless. Just as the truth of hunger cannot be read in a single expression and the truth of fealty cannot be read in a single bended knee, so the truth of discontinuity cannot be discovered in the outer pattern of any one life. What counts is that there is such a truth, and that (puzzlingly) it has in Portugal the force of revelation. The abstractions that summarize it have little power to move (who can be grief-struck because a state which opens itself to modern experience for the purpose of reenacting the past proves merely that the state too is no master of time?). Even at the very moment of confrontation with a paradox, some sign of the total manipulation of life, the throat does not sob itself sick as in adolescence, crying out: All life is a production and a stunt. But despite this, despite awareness of how swiftly a technology bent on *directing* can turn experience into a crazy drum, a fresh encounter with the two-timing does have the power to shock. And the memory of the shock persists. Long after gentle melancholy voices and the shouting sun are forgotten the mind runs back bemused to the kneeling woman never seen, that light of the Englishman's vision: whether she knelt for the President or for **Our Lady**, says the picture, all she was after on the **Merritt Parkway** was mercy, mercy from the Beaters, the Contrivers, and the idea of that, the idea of asking. . . .

A needling wonder in the brain—perhaps this is what the country is: or a souvenir miracle of some sort. Whatever the right name for it, the place is best avoided by travelers who would prefer to return not pitying us all.

1960

Pure
Politics

After thirty years of brooding, the architects of the new theoretical house of politics seem at last to be settling on a design.

Protestants all (of a sort), these figures were from the beginning in essential agreement; the mansion thrown up by nineteenth-century utopianism and social gospel was pretentiously non-functional—a chaos of gingerbread and golden oak, with a dozen chapels, infirmaries, and soup kitchens on every floor, and no room for council chambers except in the basement. And to a man they were minds of remarkable force. (Among the more famous names were Camus, Popper, Niebuhr, Hayek, and Sir Isaiah Berlin.) But neither the size of their gifts nor their readiness to assert that the old show place would have to go obviated the need for exact elevations and specifications. And only in the last decade have the latter begun to come forth.

Their key feature, as Hannah Arendt's recent writing testifies, is a conception of politics as a thing in itself—an item possessed of a unique and admirable quality which deserves inviolable shelter of its own. And the matter excluded from the new chambers, as would have been expected, is that which gave the old ones their peculiar clutter and warmth—social questions and humanitarian aspirations. Nothing is "more obsolete" now, Dr. Arendt contends, than "attempts to liberate mankind from poverty by political means"; indeed "the lesson to be derived from all revolutions that tried to solve the . . . predicament of poverty by political means [is that] nothing could be more futile or more dangerous." And from this it follows than an ideal house of politics is bare of irrelevancies, free of follies that tease the eye into mistaking abundance for freedom—a place wherein the separateness of political progress from social progress can instantly be grasped by legislators and sightseers alike.

The methods by which this design is justified in Dr. Arendt's work are both ingenious and, from a historical viewpoint, a trifle reprehensible. In her essay *On Revolution* (1963) this author re-creates three great upheavals— French, American, and Russian—on her own terms, which is to say on terms that unrelentingly emphasize the incapacity of revolutionary leaders to keep the lines clear between effort to found a new body politic, and effort at easing the misery-ridden lives of the masses. The American Revolution, as Dr. Arendt acknowledges, cannot quite be fitted to this pattern. The Founding Fathers were able to create a new body politic and to know, through that act of creation, the experience of freedom; necessity in the form of overwhelming poverty did not force them to translate political issues into social terms. But the passage of generations in America at length blurred the distinction between politics and social welfare. Once the American of middle condition became wealthy, he ceased to treat the world of politics as a place of self-realization, and thought of it merely as a helpmeet of conspicuous consumption, with the result that no post-revolutionary renewals of political energy occurred here. Elsewhere the confusion between politics proper and socioeconomic matters was evident almost from the start—and, as indicated, Dr. Arendt justifies the Purer Politics in part by dramatizing the ruinous consequences of this confusion.

The other part of her method—visible also in this author's earlier book, *The Human Condition* (1958)— depends upon the establishment of political enterprise as an exalted independent value. Dr. Arendt's responses to revolutions are governed by belief in the dignity of the aspirations that launch them, and her summaries of political ideals are offered without reductive irony. ("Freedom" is no affair of moral relativism or credit cards; it is that activity of political persuasion and decision-making which alone creates and re-creates a body politic from generation to generation. And the "free man" is not a juvenile Nietzschnik but a participator in the management of public affairs—one who, through this participation, has released his own passion for distinction, and confronted his own need to excel.) Common phrases like "public happiness" are used throughout in a manner that makes

them point at the "pleasure" of individual politicians engaged with their peers in a gorgeous pursuit. And Dr.
Arendt's intense appreciation of the political actor in his
place enables her to write with compelling sympathy,
even with a kind of love, of figures as dissimilar as
Robespierre and the signers of the Mayflower Compact.
The effect of these celebrations of the political motive is
to set almost beyond doubt the appropriateness of a house
of politics standing in solitary grandeur in the island of its
own purity.

As should be said, the author is not at every moment
absolutely convinced of the validity of the themes described. The direction of her argument for the delimitation
of politics, her responsiveness to undistracted labor at
founding new governments, would seem bound to lead
her to an uncritical version of the American Revolution—
but again and again she checks her enthusiasm, speaking
of this event as one that took place in an "ivory tower"
and had little influence, and even complaining of the
"weightlessness" of much of the Founders' thought and
prose. Her admirers read this inhibition as evidence of
an endlessly complicated mind; carpers with a respect for
history call it a sign of a sentimental desire to have politics
both ways—elegantly abstract and compassionately aware
of human problems. And the carpers are not easy to dismiss. *On Revolution* is exhilarating in its appreciations of
political action, brilliant when it is engaged in psychological analysis (the book's tour de force is a superb analysis
of attitudes toward hypocrisy during the French Terror).
The writing, which offers no jelly beans whatever to the

frivolous, is sometimes verbose and humorless, but more often is trenchant and generously demanding, and occasionally leaps high into moving tragic intensities. And, here as elsewhere in her work, the author earns awe for her capacity to body forth, page after page, without affectation, morbidity, or obliviousness, a genuinely contemporary "best self"—aware of human darkness, yet beautifully animated in its passion for light. But there are traces of arrogance, and of sterility as well, in the ideal she creates. A product of the enormous disillusionment with utopian politics, her new political edifice, although superlatively clean and well-lighted, seems likely to be exceedingly difficult to heat. And there is a sense in which it is as forbidding to men as to germs.

That "pure" political theorists, or post-political liberals, have much in common with writers whose politics is theologically oriented seems at first glance unlikely. But, surprisingly, there are significant points of contact. Walter James's *The Christian in Politics* (1962) is a historical treatise on the relations between Christianity and politics from the early Church to modern times. Although the writer, who is editor of the London *Times Educational Supplement,* concedes the politician's influence, he is ill-disposed to the notion that arguing, persuading, and legislating are ultimate modes of self-realization. He insists that "it is difficult to see how a Christian can regard politics as a human activity of the first order," and remarks about speechmaking, an activity that stirs Dr. Arendt to the heights of her own eloquence, that it "is a great stimulus to pride." At no moment in his book is it

inapparent that he is a church architect first of all, concerned that the House of God not take on the appearance
of the Houses of Parliament.

What emerges in his study of political issues in old
eras and new, however, is a version of the truism that
buildings cannot be designed in isolation from each other.
To say that the Church should not look like Parliament
is to say that Parliament should not look like the Church.
And the most powerful sections of *The Christian in Politics* are those written in support of the latter argument,
which is, in essence, an argument against Social Gospel.
Dr. James speaks of this gospel as "a secular interpretation," and claims that its roots lie not in Christianity but
in humanitarian utopianism:

The perfectionist hopes of the nineteenth century reformers,
with their grand idea of human progress (which supplied
Communism with its own hope of the earthly paradise of the
classless society and the withering away of the State), have
worked themselves into the heads of some Christians, but have
no foundations in Christianity.

Had he stopped here, his accomplishment would have
been simply that of ruling social questions out of Christianity—but he does not stop. He advances to a vision of
"evil . . . which cannot be eradicated from political action," and thereby "proves" the falseness of the hope for
redemption of any sort through politics. In the metaphor
of renovation, political theorists like Dr. Arendt might be
said to have removed the soup kitchens and brightened
the walls; religious writers like Dr. James clear away the
altars and opt for The Shabby Look—but both have the

effect of deprecating belief that social hope can be realized through politics. For the one kind of writer the enemy of that hope is economic necessity, for the other it is sin—yet neither thinks the enemy can be outstripped by politics.

Conservative minds, of course, long ago ceased worrying about which enemy is the more devastating: sin and necessity grind our aspirations with equal viciousness, on the conservative view, and a fair aim for politics, therefore, would be to teach us not to aspire. The strongest living mind of this cast is that of Michael Oakeshott, whose *Rationalism in Politics* (1962) defines politics as "attending to the arrangements of society" and hints that its chambers ought not to be more pretentious in appearance than, say, the ticket office of the New Haven Railroad at South Station, Boston. Oakeshott's papers are marked by hostility to rationalism (it is equated with ideology, technocracy, and ignorance of the past), and by the opinion that the arrangements of society are fixed in a tradition of behavior which it is the politician's duty to fathom, not to reshape.* For people who think of politics in terms of programs and goals they express mixed pity and contempt.

A writer of great literary distinction, Oakeshott manages to lend unoriginal ideas impressive dignity. His person is unvaryingly stately; his language is donnishly remote from that of the society he addresses; and his ca-

* The notion of the politician as a follower rather than as a leader comes, of course, from Edmund Burke. Oakeshott writes of politics as "the pursuit, not of a dream, nor of a general principle, but of an intimation." In 1777 Burke wrote that the "true end of legislature" is "to follow not to force the public inclination. . . ."

pacity for grave and measured development of familiar metaphor produced, in his famous Inaugural Lecture at the London School of Economics, passages that able young political scientists here and abroad have by heart:

In political activity, then, men sail a boundless and bottomless sea; there is neither harbor for shelter nor floor for anchorage, neither starting-place nor appointed destination. The enterprise is to keep afloat on an even keel; the sea is both friend and enemy; and the seamanship consists in using the resources of a traditional manner of behavior to make a friend of every hostile occasion.

The tone of these sentences is unlike the tones of Dr. Arendt and Dr. James; there is a grim hint of satisfaction in the skeptical swell, and a deliberate refusal both of tragic idealism and of Christian waspishness. But the writer, whose predecessor as Professor of Political Science at the London School was Harold Laski, plainly is of the company that seeks to purify politics of social aspiration. And his eloquence stems directly from belief in the essential nobility of the undertaking.

Not all political writing is theoretical, as everyone knows. But the theorists' efforts at purification do have a counterpart in the work of those who deal with immediate issues or engage in empirical research. Consider for example Robert Heilbroner's *The Great Ascent* (1963). This book's aim was to destroy naïve stereotypes of the underdeveloped nations; its central argument is that "democratic capitalism, as a model for economic and political organization, is unlikely to exert its influence beyond the borders of the West, at least within our lifetimes"

—in fact, "the political processes of development" are not even discussible "in an American political vocabulary." A respected economist, and a briskly persuasive writer, Heilbroner describes the economic steps that must be taken before development of any sort can occur, and the inertial forces that resist change. He notes that people living in "highly underdeveloped political environments" cannot be expected to endure sacrifice and pain—concomitants of changes in social and economic organization —except at the bidding of charismatic leaders. And he concludes that the "price of development is likely to be political and economic authoritarianism."

To repeat: *The Great Ascent* is uninterested in the theoretical implications of its assumptions about the political patterns of development. Its target is less the wishful contemporary liberal than those "powerful private voices that continue to give lip service to the pieties . . . of free private enterprise and democracy in a situation in which all too frequently both are not only totally inapplicable but would spell chaos or even retrogression." The author is certain that the "great ascent" can be achieved, provided support is forthcoming, here and elsewhere, for "enlightened executive policies" toward collectivist or even dictatorial regimes. He is convinced, as Dr. Arendt is not, that the ascent is worth achieving regardless of the price. But despite that conviction his book stands as yet another attempt to delimit politics. Adapting to its own purposes the theory of the obsolescence of efforts to "liberate mankind from poverty" by the politics of freedom, it characterizes free political institutions as obstacles to economic development. And at its center lies a conception of the

uselessness of old-style revolutionary politics that is not
out of harmony with anti-utopianism.

As for the empiricists: their contribution to functional
political architecture has been to intensify the formalist
preoccupations of political research. In older days practical political study, though wary of "general history," was
a shade more entangled in historical and partisan circumstance, a shade less eager to abstract political processes from time-bound problems and policies, than it is at
present. (Currently fashionable inquiries focus on various
governmental roles—the role of the legislative counsel of
the Congressional committee, for instance, or of the
President's Cabinet—and of the patterns of use, over long
periods, of such institutions as the Presidential press conference.)

An example of the tendencies mentioned is *Inside Politics: The National Conventions, 1960* (1962), edited by
Paul Tillett. As the title indicates, the book is by way of
being a "current events" report. In 1960 the Ford Foundation sponsored a project with the National Center for Education in Politics and the Eagleton Institute of Politics at
Rutgers, under the terms of which twenty-four university
teachers of political science were selected to attend the
1960 political conventions and write papers on their experience; the work at hand is a selection of these documents. Many of the observers have an eye for details of
trading—the exchange of the term "sit-in" for the term
"lunch-counter" during the civil-rights squabble of Republican platform writers. And some provide telling evidence that for most men the political process currently
lacks reality. (A useful paper by Aaron Wildavsky of

Oberlin notes that a common attitude among delegates was that of the spectator—"The convention is so interesting. I like to see the way things work out.") But despite their taste for particulars, the observers concentrate mainly on process, not on issues, not even on principles. The impression left is that for the insiders of *Inside Politics* the world of social consequences is, on the whole, insubstantial. Candidates are assessed solely as political technicians, never as men of conscience. ("The proceedings were smooth, the aisles were not filled with wandering negotiators, and no note of disharmony rose to meet the public eye," says the reporter about a moment of the Republican Convention that immediately followed the Nixon-engineered "sit-in-lunch-counter" trade. ". . . Richard M. Nixon had earned the right to the accolade of leadership represented by the presidential nomination.") And in assumption and tone the sense of politics communicated is dry, routinized, neutral.

Nor is it true that the stance and attitudes described are features only of group research. James MacGregor Burns's *The Deadlock of Democracy: Four-Party Politics in America* (1963), is very much a one-man enterprise, and, at that, a work which on its face is deeply concerned about legislative stalemate. Professor Burns argues that, as a result of our attempt to combine the Madisonian system of checks and balances with the Jeffersonian concept of majority rule under parties, America now bears the burden of a four-party system: the two "congressional parties," Republican and Democratic, represent interests wholly different from those of the Republican and Democratic "presidential parties." (His account of

the exacerbating points of conflict—institutional, ideologi-
cal, and electoral—between the Congressional and Presidential parties is especially shrewd and witty.) And,
after recounting the historical evolution of this system, he
offers a series of reasonable proposals—about the design
of the ballot, party membership, fund raising, Congressional leadership, and the Electoral College—aimed at
revivifying majority rule in America.

As a handbook of suggestions for professional politicians *The Deadlock of Democracy* is a valuable work.
It is not, though, a book that persuades its reader of the
urgency of issues. The author is at pains to establish
that he wishes to develop the power of both parties, conservative and liberal; his enemy, as defined in the opening
pages, is "the vast boredom with politics" that rules America; the book is engaged throughout with technical problems. Doubtless the author's purpose was not to create a
situation in which the acts of each party while it is in power
cancel out the acts of the other while it is in power. But
his absorption with pure political process implies a large
measure of sympathy for the position that identifies the
health of this process with social justice itself.

As may not go without saying, a few bookish political
voices can still be heard defending the mishmash mansion
of yesteryear in tones that suggest hostility to politics emptied of humanitarian aspiration, and impatience with
study of political process in the abstract. And not the
least curious circumstance of the present world of political thought is that the best known of these old-fashioned
voices—that of Arthur Schlesinger, Jr.—should belong to

a member of the young, glossy, super-modern Democratic hierarchy of the moment. Schlesinger's *The Politics of Hope* (1962) occasionally echoes the well-known Administration prejudice against the "messianic vision" and the "final solution." But this prejudice does not dominate it. Almost alone among recent political commentators, Schlesinger sets store by the theory of cycles (his preface thanks "John F. Kennedy for vindicating the cyclical theory of American politics"), and upholds the idea of politics as an instrument of social hope. More important, he claims that ground for resurgence of faith in that instrument is already in plain sight.

In the ears of those who are fearful that the promised machines for political living will be occupied by passive politicos in love with tragedies they might have prevented, Schlesinger's argument makes a comfortable sound. If his purpose was no more noble than to provide house-organ good cheer to the lads on the staff, his book is at least not caught up in the academic game of absolute bifurcation (politics here, social needs there), and it is a reminder of the homey, lived-in qualities of the old political hangout— before the wreckers came. But it must be said that the idiom of the politics of hope is, on the evidence of this book, a tired idiom, one that rides lazily on clichés. "Somehow the wind is beginning to change," writes the author of *The Age of Jackson*. In the sixties "Government will gain strength and vitality from . . . fresh people and new ideas." There is a "New Mood in Politics." And "the beginning of a new political epoch is like the breaking of a dam. . . ."

It is true, of course, that if politics is not religion,

neither is it poetry. That the wreckers, purifiers, and proc-ess-definers have at the moment a near-monopoly on po-litical wit and passion; that so far as writing itself is con-cerned, the mansion or cathedral seems to have dwindled of its own will into a ticket office—these facts can be as-signed more significance than they possess. But they are not meaningless. Implicit in the flaccidity of the old po-litical style is evidence that does lend weight to the cause of the reforming architects and technicians: proof, as it were, that the full aspirations of man cannot be convinc-ingly uttered now in any political language. The new-style house may never go up, old-style humanitarianism may never go out—but the likelihood is strong that not before changes occur in the literary situation of politics will any genuinely new Liberal epoch begin.

1963

The
Uses of
Anti-Americanism

Item: Balliol and Fleet St., meeting in the person of Raymond Mortimer, have denounced Yankee-hating as "a deadly sin." . . . Item: aging Angries are crying up the States freshly as a fun place (all that jazz, etc.) . . . Item: young Leavisites like Martin Green have turned pro-American and are running on (at home) about the ruddy decent-non-tenure chaps at work in our departments of Eng. Lit. . . . Item: Ian Watt, a trueborn English critic who labored for years in California, has just been brought back to the homeland to manage a revolutionary English educational institution modeled after the American "liberal arts college." . . . By the look of these and other telltales, a new English crusade against academic and literary anti-Americanism is about to be mounted: does the effort stand a ghost of a chance?

Sober Research begins its study of the question by weighing the likelihood of another Skybolt episode—another outbreak in England, that is, of public hostility to the U.S. And there is much to be said for this line of approach. Anti-Americanism is a general cultural phenomenon, something best understood in terms of overarching historical and socioeconomic considerations—as for example the truth that the American capacity to produce objects worth hating is not decreasing (you still get a lot to dislike in our boroughs), or the truth that the English capacity to restrain envy is not increasing (national peevishness is a function of national decline). Yet there are certain circumstances nurturing the growth of anti-Americanism among bookish folk that deserve to be called unique. And for that reason a sound estimate of the prospects of literary anti-anti-Americanists requires scrutiny of Yankee-hating in specifically literary terms.

The first fruit of such scrutiny, descending at once to particulars, is the disclosure that for English writers the Matter of Anti-Americanism is a valuable aesthetic resource. Not every littérateur can master the stuff, and many who could master it have found that the Matter of Pro-Americanism better suits their talents (pro-Americans tend on the whole to possess comic gifts). But the anti-American writer is a highly advantaged man. Strong appeals to his moral sensibility may induce him to undertake a re-examination of his prejudice—but the flat fact is that he cannot afford even to think of giving up that prejudice unless resources comparable to those it has developed are placed within his reach.

The resources mentioned are classifiable under four

rubrics—*Tone, Vocabulary, Genre,* and *Metaphor.* And of these four the tonal resource ranks first in importance—which is to say, the commonest bookish use of the Matter of Anti-Americanism at present is as a means of deepening one's literary voice or persona. That the literary need for such aids is acute is beyond question. Writers determined to show themselves forth as flexible, complicated men must provide themselves with issues or subjects that can be confronted in complicated ways. And in England as in America the latter are in short supply. A display of pure, or technical, intelligence is, to be sure, feasible in discussions of some contemporary issues. But few issues permit the man who addresses them to exhibit, say, responsiveness to the biddings of both head and heart, or adeptness at maintaining contradictory feelings in perilous balance. (Who but a hipster, for instance, could work out a complex position vis-à-vis the desirability of peace?) And it is precisely this sort of exhibition that the anti-American writer is superbly well situated to stage.

That the case is thus owes much to the centrality, in the anti-American matter, of a figure whose very presence has the effect of enormously complicating the feelings (and therefore the thoughts, and therefore the self-portrait) of every outsider who approaches him. This figure—call him The Exceptional American, the rose in our national dung-heap who somehow makes your fair, square English visitor stop and think—appears in various forms. His outline, like that of most stock characters in folk or mythic matter, is simple, which means that he is as pliant to journalists as the old questing knights, dying kings, talking lions, and unlucky lovers once were to poets. And he turns up

anywhere and earns his living anyhow. Francis Williams,
author of *The American Invasion* (1963), found his Exceptional Native American at the University of California,
where the fellow was working as chairman of the department to which Williams was attached during his recent
tour of duty at Berkeley. Lord Kinross, in *Innocents at
Home* (1960), found his Exceptional Native in New
York—the man was a cab driver/artist. The Exceptional
Natives discovered by Stephen Spender and Cyril Connolly in the 1950's were certain anti-American American
writers, local chaps sharp enough to hate the U.S. with
their own sacred rage. And Sir Charles Snow's Exceptional Natives are, as might be guessed, the members of
whatever American audience he happens to be addressing
on any given night.

But what counts much more than the Exceptional
American's pliancy (or, as one might venture, ubiquity) is
his capacity to stimulate inward debate in the English
writers who encounter him. For it is as a witness of this
debate that the reader comes to awareness that the speaking writer is a genuinely supple mind—someone whose
thoughts run deep and slow, a person who, confronted
with overwhelming evidence of national beastliness, nevertheless struggles with himself before accepting it as the
Whole Story. In the course of that struggle some English
writers have dramatized themselves simultaneously as
moral men and as sinners. (The poet Spender remarks
that "the American malady is a spiritual one, the com-
mercialization of spiritual goods on an enormous scale,"
and then adds—because of an encounter with an Exceptional—that "I love America.") Others have managed to

define themselves as traditionalists flexible enough to value breaks with tradition. (Kinross, who went everywhere and saw everything—Yale, Texas, other representative spots— bemoaned the lack of coherent life in "The United States of Suburbia," yet added that, through the Exceptionals, he was put in possession of "new loves, new hopes, new memories, new ideas. . . ." Cyril Connolly, whose small joke it was to speak of us as "El Dollarado," coupled with that epithet an assertion that we had "improved on" some elemental "European virtues.") And still others have found means of showing forth a nearly astonishing quality of *forgiveness*. (On his last trip through, Sir Charles, speaking to American students on the inferiority of American institutions of learning, described himself as "one who loves you very very much," and let fall, in a tone of Zosimane reconciliation, that he was thinking of coming among our midst to live after his retirement. Francis Williams described Americans as "charitable locusts," "bored," "pathetic," "adolescent," "Status-ridden," "sheeplike," "imprisoned," "conformist," and "drunk with words"—and then burst forth with the contradictory passion of Karamazov *père:* "Dear hospitable, warmhearted, nervous people, how much I like you. . . .") The matter of anti-Americanism, in short, virtually guarantees the writer who exploits it an opportunity for betraying largeness of soul.

And, as indicated, this writer earns other rewards as well. If he is the sort of man who experiences difficulty in turning swift bright phrases, he can find in the names attached to a variety of hateworthy American objects— Babytenda, BBQ, Boilermaker, Bunny, etc.—that which

will lend pizazz to any sentence, however illy contrived. If
he is mucking on with a tiresome subject, he can rouse it
to fascinating life in a minute merely by recalling an instance, relevant or otherwise, of American depravity.
(David Holbrook interrupts a sagging chapter of his *English for Maturity* (1962)—the subject is how to teach
poetry to English school boys and girls—with an exciting
summary of Eugene Kinkead's pieces on the "cowardice"
of American soldiers in Korea.) Or, if the writer is disposed to the belief that some neglected form—the Gothic
novel, perhaps—ought to be revived, he can easily find
ways of energizing it in this matter. It is probably not too
much to say, in fact, that the anti-American matter
amounts to the largest repository of terror materials now
available to the English mind. Evelyn Waugh has drawn
upon these materials to limn a land where corpses are
never planted. Kinross was inspired by a smidgen of overheard talk at "21" to posit a community—he locates it in
South Carolina—in which food for human consumption is
cooked by atomic radiation. Williams creates a world of
"casual fornication and marijuana," wherein teen-agers
never arrive home before 2:00 A.M. and high-school boys
shoot any teacher who flunks them, where grownups
"cower at home immobilized by the immense mobility of
[our] society . . ." or hide in "bi-level brunch bars,"
"Living Forums," or "mud rooms." (The *crise de terreur*
in Williams' Gothic book involves highway building in
California. A couple whose house lies in the path of a
proposed highway is evicted by moonlight and forced to
seek other shelter:

The Highways Department slapped down an order, told you the usually quite inadequate price it proposed to pay in compensation, forbade you to remove anything from either house or garden since you were being paid, however poorly, for the place as it stood so that it could cease to do so with the minimum of delay—and that was that.)

And then, finally, there is a gift of metaphor implicit in the Matter of Anti-Americanism. The value of this last gift cannot, admittedly, be stated in a word. To perceive it the outsider must work for a grasp of problems in social nomenclature—*i.e.*, What shall the Superior call his Inferior?—that does not come easily to an American. As should be said, the problems in question have only quite recently emerged in England: when the old labels of social "degree" (yeoman, churl, apprentice, gentleman, knight) lost force, replacements for them were at first easily and rapidly found. (Toward the end of the eighteenth century, for example, the Duchess of Buckingham declared that since chapel and country folk were "most repulsive and strongly tinctured with impertinence and disrespect toward their superiors," they were best spoken of simply as "common wretches that crawl the earth.") Yet with the advent of the social conscience, naming the inferiors emerged as a genuine problem. E. M. Forster met it, with humane self-mocking irony, by trusting the phrase "the very poor" ("We are not concerned with the very poor. They are unthinkable"). But when the very poor ceased to be very poor, the phrase no longer served. Miss Mitford, working from above, tried U and non-U; Messrs. Hoggart, Raymond Williams, and Wollheim, working from below, tried Them and Us—but neither effort was successful. What was wanted was a terminology which, neutral or even anthropological on its face, nevertheless would express a measure of the traditional or inherited distaste for "base mechanicals." (As Anthony Sampson of the *Observer* recently noted, the sense of class difference in England has grown more intense, not less, in the postwar era.) And it is here that the metaphorical resources implicit in anti-Americanism have performed perhaps their most brilliant service.

An inkling of the nature of this service can be gathered from Francis Williams' book. Written in an easy, meanspirited manner by an OBE, life peer, and former governor of the BBC, *The American Invasion* is, in the main, an ordinary piece of Yankee-baiting. The prime assumption of its author, who succeeded Sir Charles in a boodle appointment ("Regents Professor") at the University of California in 1961, is that America has never been an open society, and has always been coarse, crude, "conformist" in conscience. The book's moments of special piquancy occur, as hinted before, when the visitor deals with the Exceptionals who, in the homely phrase, got him into the big money ("When we were first arrived in California, the Chairman of the University Department to which I was attached, and his wife, who were to become two of the dearest friends we have known in our lives . . ."). And occasionally the author takes up the argument that gave him his title—namely that American money is buying up England. Williams notes that eight hundred American-controlled firms are now operating in his country, that the Safeway chain is about to start business there, that American investment in British industry is currently ten times higher than it was before the war, and is "increasing at an average rate of well over 13 and a half percent annually," and that as a consequence England will shortly be only another consumer-goods wasteland. ("What American business is seeking to export to Britain is not just money but American civilization and an American way of life. In an economy tied to a spiralling consumer demand this is the necessary concomitant of success.")

Standard stuff. And the details of the nightmare quality of individual American lives are also for the most part familiar. But the thesis and the details do combine to create a context in which the key metaphor in question— one that likens the English clod to the representative American—can effectively be drawn. And at the moment this metaphor is introduced, Mr. Williams rises to eloquence. His mode of approach, as should be granted, is conventional. English expressions of class prejudice have ever been accompanied by allusions to a golden age of natural noblemen: the man who announces his distaste for the working-class types of his own time invariably recalls a day when the same chaps were the salt of the earth. And Mr. Williams abides by this rule. Before speaking of the present he offers an image of Burnley in Lancashire in former days—Burnley the cotton town, full of old-style merry factory life, a place where men and women were "tough, idiosyncratic, humorous and independent. . . ." He acknowledges in manful voice that conditions of industry were "rough" in ye times, and that traces of ugliness were to be found in the back-to-back houses, but he gives it as his view that Burnley in those days was "a community in which everyone knew everyone else" and the family was "a tight, self-dependent unit." Whereas today Burnley's business is new-style light industry: the factories are "bright and clean," places where "women workers sit in bright crisp nylon overalls, doing the same thing over and over and over." Gone the charm of the back-to-back houses. Gone the challenging labor of the "weaving sheds." And gone too the feeling for the Auld Ones, the near ones and dear ones. What remains—

Here of course is the crux. What are the "remainders" to be called? To repeat, primal caste terms—"common wretches" and the like—are Out. Yet the old impulse to contempt, the incapacity to probe for the humanness that, in England or in America, resides within every living man, is still strong. (Williams scornfully remarks at one point that ". . . the majority [of the workers] are happy in their work. It leaves them with unengaged minds. They can dream while their fingers follow their intricate but repetitive patterns.") The clear task is to find terms for the inferiors that will neither outrage egalitarianism nor wholly blunt the necessary edge of scorn. And exactly these terms are implicit in The Metaphor. Mr. Williams recalls that, on his last visit to the factories at Burnley, he confronted a worker and asked her what she thought about as she worked. "My boyfriend and I going to America," was the answer. He runs on to observe not that the woman's answer expresses a tough, idiosyncratic desire that the chubby visiting guvnor arse off, but that it reveals an appalling, or echt American, emptiness of mind. He then links the answer with others offered in similar interviews ("Another [worker said:] 'I think of my new hair-do and what's on the telly and why can't we have some of those drug stores they have in America?"). And he finishes by quoting a plant supervisor who nails the case tight: "Yes, I think you could say they [the workers] are getting Americanized. . . ."

If the author of *The American Invasion* stood alone in this use of the English-clod/representative-American metaphor, he would rate praise as some kind of original genius. But of course he doesn't stand alone. A half-dozen writers have discovered that the way to put down the Other, Unwashed, non-U England is by seeing it as America. Mr. Holbrook, indeed, has even gone so far as to define whole sectors of the younger generation as, in essence, Americans, purely by looking at "literary" evidence. *English for Maturity* quotes the speech and private letters of lowly English types, items displaying tastes and idioms that are vividly, hatefully Yank: ". . . if only you were here with me to hear *Begin the Beguine* and *St. Louis Blues* on the electric guitar. . . . Oh Boy! those blues . . ." The book compares this evidence with normal English speech (Sir Walter Raleigh's letter on the eve of his execution). And then, with precisely the right mixture of sniffishness and concern, it concludes that the patterns of English life are being urged on "in the American direction."

Conceivably the anti-anti-Americanist cause will be weakened by the disclosure that the Matter of Anti-Americanism is becoming increasingly valuable as a mechanism for the expression of purely local English hostilities. Conceivably nothing less than the impossibility of a successful anti-anti-American crusade is signaled in the incapacity of English travelers to take in the simplest truth about America—namely, that the real triumph of this country lies in the creation of a society whose machinery is by no means bound to break down at the moment class feeling (the poisonous but indispensable lubricant of a smooth-running England) disappears. But neither circumstance justifies suppression of the facts. To defeat the enemy one must know the enemy: one must know, in sum, that the litry anti-Americanist who gives up his hatred gives up large resources of glamour and terror, splendid devices for the display of contrarieties of sensibility, and a metaphor that marks him off, subtly but plainly, as a traditional English gentleman. The single consoling thought, perhaps, is that while few writers will be able to afford such a sacrifice, those who can afford it will inevitably be the men who possess the richest natural gifts of the age.

1963

Letter from the Classes

Consider these people, then, their way of life, their habits, their manners, the very tones of their voice; look at them attentively . . . the things which give them pleasure, the words which come forth out of their mouths, the thoughts which make the furniture of their minds. . . .

Ninety some years ago, when Matthew Arnold's "Culture" delivered this command, the methodologists in the audience must have flipped. "Consider these people"— *how?* Following Arnold's example a researcher could ponder the published utterances of contemporary figures of *chutzpah* like Mr. Bright and Mr. Roebuck and Mrs. Gooch. Or he could take to the streets and eavesdrop on the rank and file of the local London gangs—the Philistines and Barbarians, as Arnold called them. But in either case the stuff he assembled would be junk unless worked up in historical comparisons—and how were such comparisons to be made? Where were the old documents on which to base them? Who could believe that the records of yester-year contained as much as a sneeze worth linking with the day-to-day talk of people at hand?

The problems suggested by these questions still exist, as goes without saying, but they have lately been decreasing in difficulty. Fifty years ago a Modern Language Association president, speaking on "Disrespect for Language," claimed that:

Our daily utterance we cannot, of course, measure with that of yesterday. . . . As to the written word, the hindrances of forming a correct judgment are hardly slighter.

But he himself pointed out that "Today [1911] practically everybody writes," and the prophecy implicit in this remark—namely, that a day was near when records of "the words that come forth out of their mouths" would be more complete than any hitherto imagined—has turned out to be sound. At present (and for some time past) millions of words of direct quotation from the people—observers of accidents, heavyweight contenders, magistrates, rapists, and stars—are linotyped every year. Transcripts of legislative proceedings and courthouse trials have been producing larger quantities of printed talk than are found in newspaper morgues. At one eastern college a collection of published and unpublished pollster surveys—containing interviews (circa 1920-1960) by market researchers, sociologists, political scientists, economists—fills a building capable of housing over one hundred thousand ordinary books. The existence of this matter is proof that opportunities for comparative study of "the very tones" of daily utterance over the generations are already immensely superior to those available when Culture pronounced from Arnold's knee.

Among the best of these opportunities is that provided by the alumni magazine of the American school and college. The back pages of these journals are filled with columns by class secretaries that quote postcards and letters in which men and women who were twenty-one in 1885—or 1925 or 1960—name in their own words their aspirations, activities, assumptions, and tastes.* Primitive truths of contemporary experience appear everywhere in these sheets. By turning the pages of a women's college bulletin the reader can easily follow the movement from femininity to feminism to universal gal-fridayism. With one twist of the dial he can tune to the breathlessly, managerially *chic* voice of the new woman, the voice of charm-fashion-travel copy:

Melissa (Case) and Bob Dill spent 3 wks. last winter skiing in St. Anton, Kosters and Zermatt. Lissie was *"cowed by Alps. European ski crowds and bikini-topped stretch pants—makes Stowe look like a quaint little molehill in Ozarks. South for month in Italy, met a friend and had glorious time mixing pasta and palazzos to Paestum and back via Fiat and was thankful for O'Neil's art courses. Found some wonderful angels I'm using in my Christmas '60 line."* (Class of 1948)

And by collecting references to husbands he can confirm a sense that a shared assumption of contempt for the limp

* The quotations below are drawn from the alumni magazines of two eastern institutions, a men's college and a women's college; emphasis and fictitious names have been supplied, some dates and places have been altered, but otherwise the passages are reproduced as first printed.

male only lately became a key element in the (bored) imagination of educated womankind. Here are two examples:

. . . I've been leading about as average a life as any Mrs. John Doe in suburbia with 2 children: sing in the church choir . . . solicit funds for various causes, assist with Girl Scouts, chase my 3 yr. old boy when necessary and *feed my husband a late dinner when he drags in.* (Class of 1942)

Alice (Ober) Shanahan writes that she is so exurban she has moved to Geneva, Switz., *"o.k. for people who can stand their husbands for a 2 hr. lunch every day."* (Class of 1947)

Snippets read in isolation yield inklings, of course, not Ford Foundation conclusions: to produce the latter an investigator would need to compare idioms in instances of similar "life situations." But that enterprise itself is by no means impossible. A Long Island minister, secretary of the class of 1892, observes that:

It is sixty-nine years since we stood in the gallery and sang, "Lord of all being throned afar," and heard President Boylston pray.

And the observation becomes evidence of a sort about the modern development of the religious sensibility when it is compared with the remark of a New Jersey minister of the class of 1945:

I've been getting my feet on the ground, hope to get more chance to hob-nob with fellow alumni and sing something other than hymns.

And even when "life situations" cannot be specified, an unrigorous eye turns up suggestive details—on subjects ranging from the changing styles of nostalgia to the evolution of the educated man's joke—in almost every issue. In the men's college class of 1899 *memory* expresses itself thus:

. . . remember how we used to rush headlong up to Chapel? Remember also the two flights of stone steps we had to climb to get to the gallery? . . . Do you recall the staid old pictures adorning the walls? Do you also recall Old Hal's prayers—how he talked directly and earnestly to and with the Lord, using "You" entirely and not "Thou" and "Thee"? . . . Remember blind Professor Knowles "reading" long passages from the Bible and not missing a single word? [Do you remember] where good old Bobby Crowell presided, Bobby Crowell who made Latin a living language and the ancient Roman heroes everyday acquaintances? Bobby the modest scholar and the well-bred gentleman—one of the best.

In the class of 1945 memory expresses itself thus:

I still laugh thinking of picture-taking efforts at the strip tease palace in Chicago. Camera under the tablecloth—remember?

In the class of 1892 an accepted mode of teasing a classmate is the following:

One man sent the Secretary his generous contribution to the Alumni Fund. He hopes it arrived at the College.

In the class of 1943 the modes of teasing are a shade broader:

Our busiest classmate last year was undoubtedly Cal Church. His biggest accomplishment was getting married to Maria Sloss in Washington, D.C. on June 15, 1956. The new couple are residing in a Philadelphia suburb . . . where they are anxiously awaiting their first born, due in *April*. . . . Congratulations, Cal, when you take a plunge, you go in with both feet! You may be a late starter, but it appears that you'll soon close the gap!

Items even more trivial than these gain an edge of meaning as the language of one generation is related to that of another. A non-ironical clutch of metaphors from 1945 bespeaks the advent of a cheerfully clichéed blankness:

. . . busy as a bee, working like a dog keeping the wolf away from the door.

A specimen of homemade rhetoric from 1889 has a tougher ring:

Refrain from loquacity/Be crisp and concise/And regard self-pity/As a cardinal vice.

Shifts in tone concerning such subjects as the turning of years tell a comparable tale. A member of the class of 1891 quotes words of humor and grace:

A remark made by [your Secretary's] father at the first Thanksgiving dinner from which all his children were absent applies equally to the '91 survivors: "At any rate, Charlotte, we may be thankful that we cannot be cut off in youth."

While on the same subject 1935 is paunchy and raucous:

Our class baby . . . is graduating this year. Makes you feel old, eh? Well brother just look in the mirror.

Describing his residence, a member of the class of 1892 lets fall that he is happily situated *"rus in urbe,"* while 1944 takes his audience inside:

Ours is a do-it-yourself saltbox on a 6 acre hunk of Adirondack-type land only 21 miles from Grand Central Station.

After utilities (involving 6 poles), 800 feet of road and laying a water line mostly through rock, there wasn't enough jack . . . left in the till for a garage. We do have an inside head, though, literally built around a 4 foot Italian marble sink, discarded when Rockefeller modernized the plumbing in the big house. . . .

And in the matter of comparative jokes the nineteenth-century classes run to rural fables about Uncle Ezra and Uncle Dudley, while more recent graduates favor items like the following:

One suggestion for costumes for our 25th [reunion] was that Pat Harvey make up some atomic brassieres for our lovies to wear. You know—75 per cent fallout.

If the larger patterns visible in these records contradicted the suggestions gleaned by comparing snippets, the latter would hardly be of account. But there are no contradictions. The step backward from specific entries to general contrasts not only strengthens the impression of a freshening tide of vulgarity, but it puts before the reader the possibility that in these times the notion of youth as complication and age as simplicity is not less than wholly false. Advancing with the classes from 1885 to the present means exchanging voices of interest, complicated natures in which wit, gentleness, pride, and irony are brought together, for reports from nothingness like the following:

Troubles galore for Bill Kevin and Ad Henry. Their Pittsburgh plant . . . has been on strike for over five months . . . with a good possibility that it will be closed indefinitely. Ad as vice-president in charge of sales hasn't had much to sell, but in spite of that competition has been reducing prices. Bill went to Florida to forget his troubles, but ruptured a disc in his back hauling in a big one.

Are these impressions simply a matter of what is called style? The typical reporter of the nineties does possess an odd turn of speech, at once careless and elegant, formal and teasing. "Burgess," he may write (approaching his ninetieth year), "Burgess seems to have no objection to running for the notable honor of the presidency. . . . He rather intimates [in addition] that your Secretary is not asleep." He is fond of the third person singular, indirect discourse, Latin tags, and complicated jokes. He likes to telescope time, and the sentences in his columns, which dart without signal from generation to generation, make a pleasant demand of agility on his readers. But he sometimes ends a piece with an afterthought in which the distance between his classmates' present and past is named with a sudden touch of glory—as in the sentence quoted earlier:

It is sixty-nine years since we stood in the gallery and sang, "Lord of all being throned afar," and heard President Boylston pray.

But proclaiming that the differences in question are "mere" matters of idiom won't finally do: there is more to the voice of the nineties than queer syntax. Consider the acting secretary of 1892. The fellow has about him on the one hand an attractive acidity; it appears when a classmate invites him to moralize:

Hall asks [says the acting secretary], Why is it that you and I who never drank a drop or smoked a smoke live on forever and so many of our more "convivial" classmates pass on? In answer . . . note that frequently some centenarian asked the reason for his longevity [replies] that he drank a quart of whiskey every day, and, further, perhaps the acting secretary has been more convivial than Edward Hall knows.

But the same man is frequently moved by a commemorative impulse. Over the years he recounts a dozen acts of kindness with a light simplicity that does not hide quickness of feeling. He recalls in one column that:

On May 27, 1890 [the secretary] attended the Intercollegiate Athletic Meeting when we won by a large margin over Dartmouth and six other colleges, though we were amazed in the morning at being beaten in football by Stagg's team, 18 to 4, with Stagg himself . . . grinning on the sidelines. At noon I entered a crowded restaurant. I was working off my tuition at fifteen cents an hour in the College Library, had not enough money to join a fraternity. In that restaurant Old Hal Creston [a professor], most beloved for a generation, who gave me the first overcoat I ever owned, put his arm over my shoulder and said, "Doyle, let us see if we can't get some dinner." So I dined with Old Hal.

The reporter just quoted had occasion once to write a notice about the death of his own son. The item was placed well down the text of the column, and qualified as an admirably poised little piece of writing, humane and considerate in its control of the emotions of pride and loss:

Reverend Richard Ball Doyle, D.D., according to a *New York Times* notice January 2, died in his sleep in ——, California, January 1, with notes for the sermon he planned to preach January 2 on the night-stand beside his bed. In 1940 he took the church with 1350 members and he left it with 4300 members. He leaves a wife and three children as well. He was fifty-two years old.

And an obituary on a valued friend is not less admirable at its close, where after six weighted impersonal paragraphs, the writer steps quietly forward to speak his whole conviction:

God loved him—and so did all of us. He received his Coronation, for of such is the Kingdom of Heaven.

From impressions of the sort offered here no conclusion should be drawn, perhaps, save that they are impressions, and that a man who let them stand as powerful evidence of decline would deserve chiding on several grounds. The famous phrase does say, after all, that style is the ultimate morality of the mind, and whether or not *ultimate* is the key word, people who graduated in 1892 plainly are older than people who graduated in 1945.* What is more, the assumption that style is the man, or that modes of expression equal ways of feeling, or that tones of voice are in all cases synonyms for manners and behavior is itself open to criticism. And again: the majority of the characters who went to college in 1890 unquestionably occupied a position in society unlike that of the majority of the applicants in the age of Merit Scholarships and reverse-snob Ivy admissions offices. But this barrage of qualifications and hesitations doesn't quite make ashes of the old bidding of Culture quoted before. Conceivably the idea of ripeness and fullness of character can survive anything,

* There is little to suggest, however, that the idiom in which the classes of the nineties speak is a product of great age: the manner of speech recorded in the notes of these classs in 1960 is not essentially different from that recorded in the notes of classes thirty and forty years ago.

even the loss of telling models. But the survival is not a certainty, and Culture's command probably should now at long last be obeyed—by idlers or researchers or any others with ears to hear and compare "the words that come forth," the tones and the thoughts which, in an age of uncertain selves, make the furniture of the general mind.

1961

Statement and Struggle: A Note on Teaching Against the Environment

> The truth is, we must often struggle and always be pre-
> pared to struggle . . . to keep alive [the] inherent sense
> for what is lively and good in art. How to conduct this
> battle joyously, in such a way that we will . . . not alien-
> ate [people] from the life of the mind, is a problem which
> it may take genius to solve.
>
> *Isaac Rosenfeld*

Why a struggle? Why a battle? Why a tortuous problem requiring Mind? Only among the innocent do the
questions still arise. It is known that the dragon Masscult
has uncounted tongues, and that whenever one is sheared
—whenever a bad book, say, receives a stern just notice in
the *Times Book Review*—two or a dozen nastier fangs
flame out instantly in its place. It is also known that the
standards once confidently invoked by the dragon's quon-

dam foe, the literary humanist, have lately been sapped of authority by historicism. ("Popular art is normally decried as vulgar by the cultivated people of its time," says Northrop Frye, speaking in the new historicistic tone, "then it loses favor with its original audience as a new generation grows up; then it begins to merge into the softer lighting of 'quaint,' and cultivated people become interested in it; and finally it begins to take on the archaic dignity of the primitive.") It is clear in addition that the simple terms in which matters such as the size of the potential audience for good work were once discussed—terms that link taste and class—are no longer useful or even relevant. (In the world of entertainment, as Raymond Williams soundly remarks, "the masses" and "the minority" are models constructed and manipulated by powerful entrepreneurs, "models which in part create and reinforce the situation they apparently describe.")

That intellectuals and teachers are increasingly conscious of the complexities of the problem does not mean, however, that they have a clear understanding of the obstacles to their own efforts at coping with it. Available critiques of individual popcultural depravities (from *Playboy* to the *National Geographic*) and compilations of economic facts about massification (from the break-even point for first novels to the required capitalization for a new daily paper in New York) are, to be sure, of some help. They establish on the one hand that contention for the lively and good in literary art isn't simply contention against profit, Henry Luce, and comma faults, but against certain kinds of experience whose attractions must be grasped in general terms—*readers'* terms. And on the other, these critiques strengthen belief that the likeliest challenger of the dragon is indeed education in the large —education "against the environment," education functioning as the champion of good literary experience against bad. But they do not clarify the nature of the forces inhibiting teachers from becoming challengers. If it is true that sooner or later every popculturist finds himself imagining an ideal warfare between the academy and *kitsch,* it is also true that most of the tribe avoid the question why the outbreak of actual hostilities has been so long postponed. And until that question is answered, the likelihood is small that challengers will emerge.

Part of the answer, naturally, is far from recondite. The inhibiting agents in academe include the tide of relativism just mentioned, the normal institutional fear of antagonizing any segment of the mass-communications industry, the normal haughtiness of teachers whose first concern is for literature, not the quality of national life. But beyond these items lies a grand turn of intellectual history—a development that by a paradox can be seen as determining the peculiar qualities of the new subliterary reading experience, as well as the peculiar timidities of littérateurs. The pursuit of this paradox is at every moment in danger of flying up into super-subtlety; and the "explanation" of pedagogical reticence that it suggests appears at first glance abstract. Nonetheless, the classroom situation that is shaped by the terms of the paradox is for the teacher not less than disablingly real.

*

As might be assumed, an attempt to characterize this situation requires the restatement of some commonplaces about popular "reading matter" and masscult-midcult style. To speak of style is not to insist that the only appropriate context for scrutinizing the commercial literary culture is formal. Popular taste has a sociology as well as an ideology; the world of glossy pages is a holiday world not solely because of its manner, but because it is untainted by purposefulness: no school, business, or government has turned it into Work. Neither is it to claim that the content of the glossy page (fantasies of sex, success, fame, and adventure) is without significance as a lure. It is to say that the holiday world of commercial culture is marked by a number of formal constants (tones, rhetorical patterns, dramatic stances) that offer one key to both its unity and its attractiveness.

Prime among these constants is the stance of non-assessment. Throughout mass- and midcult, the accepted rhetoric condemns the authoritative or judicial voice and disapproves undramatized summary—"undramatic" meaning here simply didactic. The prejudice named has not, needless to say, swept away all editorialists and silenced all moralized song. When college boys descend from bars (at 3:00 A.M. of a Labor Day morning) to the streets of an upstate New York resort (shouting, singing, and tossing beer cans through plate-glass windows), the coverage provided by newspapers and news magazines does not aim at neutrality. When young wives set down (in letters to ladies' magazines) fierce grievances against lazy, unloving spouses, the editorial voice that answers does not strive for a permissive or sympathetic tone. When a blow is struck at a revered upper-middle-class convention or standard, magazines like the *New Yorker* do not report the news acceptingly. And (descending to a lower level), when confession magazines tell of some celebrity whose home has broken in divorce, their remarks are not commendatory.

What counts in sustaining the holiday experience, though, is that masscult reproof is no matter of a straightforward summarizing judgment. The "light reading" of the sixties spares its audience the disturbance of an editorial voice speaking with an air of comprehension or inclusiveness. Its statements are distributed statements. They are not concentrated in paragraphs severe with assumptions about duty and responsibility. And their effect is to assign the task of naming the meaning of events, not to the editor (or to the journal itself), but to a character in the scenario—or to the reader himself. Thus *Time* doesn't in its editorial persona define beer-can hurlers as depraved youth; it closes its report on delinquency with a remark of a distant policeman. ("This is typical of what we're up against," said Captain Jim Glavas of the Los Angeles police department's juvenile division, "a complete disregard for everything—you can't give a reason for it. It seems to be a national malady. The standards seem to have disappeared, and we have kids without standards.") The case for gentillesse and old-fashioned manners, on the tennis court and elsewhere, is not argued by the voice of the *New Yorker* speaking in the "Talk of the Town"; it is instead reported, wrapped in quotation marks, and offered as the rumination of the codger or the long-winded old lady "who sometimes writes to us." The *Ladies' Home Journal* does not answer the women who think ill of their husbands; instead it prints a fourteen-point test of expectations ("Check the qualities below that you want your husband to have") that the reader herself can take, and from which she may or may not rise with the conviction that in the past she has expected too much. The magazine of confessions absolutely refuses to provide a summary in place of "experience"; its first-person narratives ("When Divorce Split My World") are designed to thrust the reader into immediate situations. "When Faye and I faced the grim fact that our marriage could not be saved," runs the lead sentence of the agony of Doug McClure in a recent *True Confessions,* "we didn't expect it to be easy on us. The one person we were worried about was our little girl, Tane."

Adaptations or dabblings in this mode are numberless. The voice of the commercial ("I love you, Wolfschmidt" —"Marge, it's a white tornado!") is not that of the manufacturer; the voice of the opinionated essayist is represented by publishers (in subtitles) as that of an impersonal Report; the voice of the New York *Times* editorial page competes with an italicized box "featuring" a "Quotation of the Day." And, as should be acknowledged, a measure of the enthusiasm for the new mode is traceable simply to its convenience for writers and editors. These men know that formulating opinions, marshaling evidence, and organizing arguments convincing on their own terms is hard labor; and, in any case, they are eager to present themselves as modest unlitigious types, aware of the inevitable partiality of any single understanding of affairs.

In the present context, however, the figure of interest isn't the writer but the reader. His situation, as indicated,

is holiday-like partly because the reading bazaar belongs
to an unpurposeful fun-world, but also because the bazaar
appears unconcerned with "pushing" conclusions, sum-
monses, or demands. The "lightness" of his pleasures is
guaranteed by the vocabulary, the subjects, and the text-
photograph ratio of his reading matter, but also by its tone
and dramatic stance: the scenarios do not "come out,"
judgment itself is represented as stage business, assess-
ments of experience are mere snippets of dialogue, beats
in the dramatized "rundown of events." Rapt in plasti-
scene as it were, the reader can transcend the plane of
quarrel and conflict, and enter an airy undemanding world
in which the proper response to any assertion, any summary, is not Yes or No but, rather, "That's what he said."
He may if he wishes smile at the police officer ruminating
on the decay of standards—a simple uneducated man,
probably sees a lot of ugliness, groping for the answer—
but to seize such openings seems an act of pedantry. Why
quarrel with a Los Angeles cop? Does he rule the world?
That question, endlessly repeated (What is this voice to
me?) habituates readers to non-response. The unpreten-
tiousness of the summarizing remark—the obvious simplicity and candor—silences reservations: "—a lot in
that," says the reader with a shrug, and the page is turned.

It is this succession of turnings and voices that creates
an audience, a crowd of spectators conscious of experience only as a show not to be interrupted—a flow
of events, remarks, events, remarks, the motion of which
cannot be stopped, held fast, examined. We are "there,"
on the scene, but not responsibly, individually there, not
there to be lectured at or convinced or asked to make up

our minds. The world is dense with decisions, to be sure, everyone talking, deciding, valuing. But the decisions are overheard, not addressed to us: this world does not talk back, it asks nothing, it lets its eavesdroppers drift down and down through column on column of happenings into a sweet, easing unresponsiveness—even into wordlessness itself.

So much is familiar. And on its face it would seem unlikely in the extreme that the teacher concerned with educating against the environment would be badly placed for contention. The pattern of such contention virtually shapes itself. Aware that criticism of the environment requires acknowledgment that an environment exists, the teacher begins by admitting the bad and the unliving into his classroom, where he subjects it to examination. His aim is to demonstrate that the twin effects of drama-*kitsch* are to disguise opinion and to repress argument. In working toward this goal, he employs methods once tentatively approved by the schools in the thirties and forties—for ventures in "propaganda analysis." That is, he points at moments in his exhibit when readers are in fact obliquely moralized at, hectored, teased into one or another position. And at the crisis of his exposition, he names the elements of anti-life implicit in the indirection at hand, and undertakes to establish that the reader who collects the parts of the distributed summary and brings their meaning to consciousness would arrive at an intuition of the cost of his holiday.

The apparent ease and reasonableness of this undertaking, though, are delusive, in large measure because the act of comparison just mentioned exacts a sacrifice to Statement that is considered offensive to taste and tact. It is precisely here that the connection between *kitsch* obliquity and academic non-combativeness appears. The holiday ideology of taste, with its eschewal of direct summary or crystallization, is actually a consequence of the revolution in the name of the dramatic that was fought and won generations ago in high culture. But the non-commercial inheritors of that revolution, men who regard it as a stroke for truth rather than for profit, are themselves as fully in its thrall—which is to say, as wary of crystallization—as are the men of commerce. On elevated grounds they have turned hostility to the didactic or non-dramatic view of life into a positive value; they see the summarizing critic, the man who attempts to translate a story or poem from its own terms into those of moral discourse, as one who dishonors the shrine of art. And in their minds the act of isolating an anti-life position in one text and of comparing and contrasting it with a different position in another text is at best senseless and at worst a deceit.

As should be acknowledged, the sanctification of the dramatic cannot be thought of as a pointless aesthetic foible or accident: it constituted (at the end of the last century) an earnest response to an impressive series of developments in the history of science, faith, and society. The familiarity of the tags that in one fashion or another abuse the non-dramatic ("Do not tell, show"—"Trust the tale, not the teller"—"A mind so fine that no idea could violate it"—"We hate poetry that has a design on us") is evidence in itself that for literary men this tradition is now dominant. The hero who validates the mode, Henry

James, is ever more clearly seen as the most potent re-
former of taste since Coleridge. And it is past doubt that
this writer's struggle against simplistic unearned pontifica-
tion was waged in the service of a noble end, that of
civilizing a nation out of its crudities of judgment and into
a moral awareness adequate to the complexity of human
affairs.

When all this is said, however, there is substance in the
claim that the effect of the victory has been to weaken the
hand of teachers resolved to contend against bad literary
experience. Such men may give assent to the proposition
that every good poem is a criticism of bad poetry, but they
are usually slow to set forth such critiques in their classrooms. The article of their deepest faith is that an unmistakable badge of teacherly vice is the determination to
utter summary statements, willingness to concentrate on
what Graham Greene speaks of as "the moment of crystallization where the dominant theme is plainly expressed,
when the private universe becomes visible even to the least
sensitive reader."

I read somewhere [writes a Leavisite of considerable moral
fervor, intelligence, and concern for public matters] an apoc-
ryphal story about the composer Schumann who was asked
the "meaning" of one of his pieces of music. In answer he
played it again. And when the questioner repeated his question, he played it again. The piece of music *is* the meaning:
the poem, as Gertrude Stein might say, is the poem is the
poem is the poem. [David Holbrook, *English for Maturity,*
1962.]

The passage is perfectly characteristic of the literary bias
here described. The poem *is* the meaning—hence, never

restate or summarize it, never fall victim to the vulgarity of hunting the Message.

The argument that this bias incapacitates teachers and critics for the struggle as defined by Rosenfeld in the epigraph above can be put too strongly. The teacher isn't altogether powerless: he can ask his classroom to "feel the life" in one exhibit and the unlivingness in another— and if he is a brilliant teacher, with a work of high art in hand, he can suggest—all obliquity and drama himself— the nature of the fullness to which he is responding without "other words." To the argument that ordinary students gain from such moments a *frisson* rather than an instrument of interrogation suitable for their own use, it can be said first that no instrument and no pedagogy yet contrived are proof against fools; and second, that to operate in more direct fashion (to compare, baldly, the good and the bad, the quick and the dead) is to waste hours in gossip. The "Epithalamion" of Spenser "as opposed to" the fourteen-point quiz in the *Ladies' Home Journal* on "What I Want My Husband To Be"—could such a class be endured? ask the enemies of Statement. Should the schools ever give houseroom to students who need to be told why the poem is "better" than the test? Is it not more sensible to keep "their" innerness and uncertainty decently hidden under the stone? Does the teacher of literature actually harm anyone by pretending that those who leave his classroom, packing a copy of Pope or Yeats, have some other destination than a mail table piled high with *Gent* and *Mad* and *Time*?

The questions have their force, as is apparent, but they fail to quiet every doubt. The iamb, the trochee, the song of the vowels, the shape of metaphor, the relation between speaker and audience—these are matters about which it is assumed, in the world of masscult-midcult, that students will not be richly informed. Given this assumption, it is perhaps not eccentric to conclude that matters of statement and meaning are equally obscure. Training in such matters, moreover, needs to go beyond the quick Lawrentian tags set in vogue by Dr. Leavis. Of course the fourteen-point text is "anti-life," but does that phrase reverberate in the student mind? Would it lose its force if amplified? ("Here is a mechanization of human relations, a turning outward into public formulae of matters that if felt at all can only be felt inwardly; if my choice is truly my choice, then it cannot be framed in fourteen queries for three million readers, pencils in hand.") Of course, the policeman's observation about "kids without standards" is anti-life: but does that phrase itself have any meaning until the hostility it objects to is understood?

The danger, that of vapid moralizing, is clear enough. But surely a terror of moralizing is not a value in itself; nor is summary that radiates the life of a text a crime. "Mr. James presents you with the proposition, not so much that there are no such things as oppressors and oppressed, but that, even in the act of oppressing, the oppressor isn't having a very much better time than his victims." This remark of Ford Madox Ford is scarcely empty for the student whose "assignment" is James's *Portrait of a Lady*: it helps, it tells him where he has been, what truth the drama earns. The habit of deprecating the gift of naming such truths is probably not the key obstacle in the path of those who seek to bring the struggle for the lively and good into the university classrooms. Yet, considered as a handmaid to obliviousness, a prop to the teacher who is bored with struggle, it does matter. Once caught in the habit, the teacher loses his own consciousness that the difference between *kitsch* and its opposite is not finally that between holiday and every day, but between a world falsified, distanced, and dried out, and a world treated, as Conrad put it, "with the highest kind of justice." It is on the wider diffusion of exactly this consciousness that all serious hope for better audiences rests.

That hope, it should be added, is currently a shade less wan than might be supposed. In England a trio of capable observers, Richard Wollheim, Richard Hoggart, and Raymond Williams, has been laboring in various ingenious ways to complicate the relations of high and low culture, and to blunt the bifurcating forces that support superstitious classifications ("easy" versus "difficult," "pretentious" versus "unpretentious," Them—the higher-ups—versus Us). In America certain elite schools and colleges have lately undertaken to confront specific productions in popular culture directly, with the aim of deciphering their "statements" and subjecting the latter to open assessment. And (more to the immediate point) there have been signs in recent days of a critical impatience with worship of the dramatic mode (witness the argument of Wayne Booth's *Rhetoric of Fiction*)—an impatience that might well issue in less embarrassment about "messages."

To hold that the latter hope is at the moment the soundest is not to withdraw the argument for contention. There are purposes to be served by confronting the bad and the unliving in the classroom; the sight of contempt for the cheap and meretricious is not always an ugly or a useless sight; the student who commits himself to the investigation of some popcultural lie hasn't necessarily polluted his mind. To repeat, the spirit of such enterprises *is* combative; poems and stories do breathe easiest in unembattled air; and, returning to the beginning, Isaac Rosenfeld surely was correct in asserting that the struggle needs to be conducted "joyously." What seems probable is that when teachers are free again to love the earned truths as well as the texture of what they teach, they will be less exacerbated by a sense of an overwhelming challenge evaded. At that moment true contention, successful struggle, may just conceivably begin.

1963

The Little
Red Discount
House

About a year ago the American Council of Learned Societies and Educational Services Incorporated began circulating a sheaf of mimeographing entitled "Preliminary Draft of a Proposal for the Support of a Curriculum Development Program in the Humanities and Social Sciences." The aim of the agencies was to win support for a new project for the reform of elementary and secondary school teaching. The reformers were, to a man, reputable academics—social scientists, historians, and teachers of literature—and their "Preliminary Draft" contained matter of interest to a variety of observers. For foundation men there were enticing work schedules and modest budgetary estimates. For scientists there was pleasing testimony that the people in the other culture were docilely following the patterns developed by mathematicians and physicists in improving instruction in their fields. (First a summer meeting of professionals to frame new approaches to old subjects; next a joint effort by university, secondary, and elementary teachers to produce textbooks embodying the fresh ideas; thereafter experimental testing of the texts in classrooms, a summer of intensive revision, national publication of the texts, and finally the institution of retraining programs for teachers committed to the use of the new books.) And for the idle gossip there were a few amusingly discussible appendices—a self-teasing glossary of terms favored by the reformers at their meetings ("INTERDISCIPLINARY—a state devoid of discipline in which it is permissible to interrupt whoever is speaking"), a page or two on the best way of teaching reading and writing which concluded, with winning embarrassment, that "reading and writing is best self-taught" (the banger of this soft drum was Professor Mark Harris).

As the appendices suggest, the reformers were at pains to avoid the ordinary styles of educational crusade. Eschewing the rhetoric of light-bringing, they presented themselves simply as people engaged in creating "specific units" that might be "spotted through the elementary curriculum or that might be considered as forming a network as they are tested and more are added." They offered no rationalization of their programs, and seemed mainly bent upon establishing themselves as easy riders. But despite all the engaging self-deprecation, a revolution plainly was implicit in their work. Examination of the "units" offered as samples disclosed that their primary goal was nothing less than a direct encounter between the childish mind and intellectual themes at once powerful and

unfamiliar to the elementary or secondary classroom—
items that could not have been settled upon merely in hope
of stimulating the teacher's ingenuity. The themes in
question—the relation between a person's interest and his
perspective, the necessity of understanding a point of view
as an agent of deflection—retain, to be sure, little grandeur
or elegance when adapted to the requirements of Innocence. (One unit called for the teacher to introduce
"tape record narratives of the same football game by a
television announcer, a sophomore girl, the winning coach,
the losing coach, the left guard's mother, and an eight
year old brother of one of the players. Tie these in [the
instructions went on] with movies or photographs . . .
to further illustrate what each person is seeing at specific
points throughout the game. This illustrates 'selective perception'—the idea that a person's point of view or 'role'
influences what he sees.") But the homeliness of the material did not alter the fact. The apparent center of the
ACLS-ESI program was the conviction that the time has
come for the ground themes of modernity to be sounded in
every glassy corner of the American public school.

That representatives of disciplines not usually pleased
with each other were able to arrive at this decision without
vicious quarrel isn't impossible to explain. Historians as
well as social scientists have caught glimpses of Marx,
Frazer, Freud, and the other giants who held that beliefs
and ideas are gestures of competing interests, that the god-
term itself is culture-bound, that no man's unprobed word
is to be trusted. And while only a few of the great literary
heroes of the century have been notable discounters, great
hordes of MLA members nevertheless stopped buying

books—*i.e.,* points of view—at list long before Korvette's turned to literature for loss leaders. The principles behind the reverse price-fixing among litry folk were tricky and exacting. (So much off the overt argument of any book for roles and points of view, as a matter of course—but then beyond this, so much off for rationalization, repression, the lessons of the symbols, imaginative designs, private vocabularies, a dozen similar cues to interest.) Yet the principles were well regarded. The case is, indeed, that contemporary academics in virtually every field became habituated long ago to the idea of selective perception—which is to say that the success in recovering a sense of the notion fresh enough to breathe humor into schoolbooks qualifies as an act of historical imagination.

There are, however, other acts to be performed before the entry of the notion into red schoolhouses and junior highs can rouse more than guarded satisfaction. It is clear that perspectivism is a splendid resource of the mind—a strong defense against ideology and fanaticism, a first-rate incentive to subtlety, complication, and (possibly) acceptance of otherness. It is no less clear that training people up from toddlerdom in this way of thought is altogether feasible. And it is likely that most of the old humanist charges against the discounters—as for example that in multiplying viewpoints they obscure values—will before long strike old humanists themselves as lacking in pertinence to the age. (In the past the charges were most popular, in any event, among observers who, when asked straight off where they took *their* stand, preferred not to commit themselves "at this time.") But when these concessions are made, it remains true that perspectivism is itself a mode of expression, and, as such, an agent of interest, an instrument of repression, a potion best cut with a cautionary word. The thinker who seizes on the new mode of thought as his mode (whether in the name of the giants, or merely in the name of wit as defined by T. S. Eliot) needs to study it negatively for a moment—in order to find out precisely what happens when the stuff of his *own* particular learning is no longer bought at full price. Failure to do this means advocating a "sensible scaling-down" of all intellectual claims, while consciously or unconsciously exempting one's own claims from sacrifice. And that way lies megalomania.

In the discipline of literature the best current laboratory for scrutiny of the effects of "discounting for viewpoints" is found in the writings of the school of Kenneth Burke. No literary theorist of the century has done more than Burke to acquaint students of imaginative writing with the implications of the perspectivist revolution.* In his early books (*Counter Statement, Attitudes Toward History, Permanence and Change*), as well as in the treatises on Motives, the now retired sage of Bennington argued with endless inventiveness for the necessity of Seeing Around the spoken or written word, the announced intention, the "successful" enterprise in persuasion—in order to register the extent of the wordman's probable deflection from the X that is not words. The argument was never simple in its assumptions. It neither groveled in the slough of logical positivism nor aspired to faith in a truth Out There, wait-

* Other students as well. *Permanence and Change,* for example, is often recommended as a work indispensable for beginners in social sciences. See C. Wright Mills's *The Sociological Imagination.*

ing to be discovered by the steely mind stripped of all deflectors. It held firm instead to a spiky set of contrarieties: language deflects and interest determines (in part) the nature of the deflection: every definition creates a situation; my definition, hence my situation, may or may not be yours; another vocabulary can always be imagined; there is virtue in "perspective by incongruity" and danger in "temporalization of essence"; society as a community of meanings, a catalogue of created scene-act ratios, continues to exist. Always, though, the theorist's eye (no flatterer) was on the limits of the strategies composed and the positions upheld. You must track down the symbols in order to find the meaningful—*tic*. ("The poet . . . squints or jerks when some words are spoken, otherwise not. You disclose the 'symbolic organization' of his tic when you have found the class of words that provokes it.") You must discount not only for the form of the expression but for the moment of biographical and historical time ("Often you cannot take a sentence at face value [you do not 'understand the meaning' until you know the biographical or historic context subsumed by the speaker when he spoke it"]). And you cannot allow an unmixed motive to stand ("a 'comic' term for the essence of motivation . . . expects an act to be moral, and it expects the actor to 'cash in on' his moral assets"; "in keeping with our distrust of both 'perfectionist' and 'invertedly perfectionist' motivations, we should feel justified in never taking at its face value any motivational reduction to a 'simple.' ")

The body of writing Burke has built up on these principles is prized on several grounds. It is first of all the

work of that rarest of men, a good-humored original
genius. It is equal to the age, conversant with ranges of
intellection unheard of by most littérateurs, impatient
with elegant, self-indulgent ignorance. It is free of fairy
aestheticism, fully responsive to the continuum of human
activity, quick to perceive ventures in order-making wherever they occur, disinclined to profundum about the
separateness of life and art. And finally, unlike most
criticism, it is generous to its reader; it tells him he has an
active mind, is agile and quick, relishes complication, is
scornful of emotional posturing and human enough to enjoy being silly now and then. As the chief critical end-
product of perspectivism it is, in short, superb testimony
that the influence of the idea can be humane.

But of course—to round on virtues in the desiderated
manner—the theories and the theorist have limits of their
own. As should be admitted, attempts to name these
limits in political or literary terms have usually come off
badly. The best remembered of them are those of Sidney
Hook and R. P. Blackmur. The former made his complaint
in a famous *Partisan Review* episode of the late thirties; he
condemned Burke as "an apologist . . . of the latest piece
of Stalinist brutality" (the Moscow trials), claiming that
Attitudes Toward History sought to rationalize in "basic
metaphors and psychoanalytic myths" deeds and necessities
of the totalitarian state that were "too stark and bloody"
to be rationalized. The latter made his complaint in "The
Critic's Job of Work"; its point was that the perspectivist's
method broke down all distinctions and could be applied
"with equal fruitfulness to Shakespeare, Dashiell Hammett,

or Marie Corelli." Both charges imply that Burke is an insensitive man—oblivious at once to brutality in life and excellence in art—and the implication is false. But, to the extent that Burke's accusers were not merely repeating mechanical formulae, they were responding to a central quality of his writing—the quality of imperviousness. And it is this quality, this set of the perspectivist being, that rouses distrust even in sympathetic observers aware of the pivotal place of resistance in the ruling strategy of the whole.

As goes almost without saying, the modes of imperviousness—the term means: rigid disbelief in the possibility of direct encounter, obstinate standing off of any and all "descriptions," refusal to accept the other man's metaphor, tone, or joke—are as various as the subjects Burke has attacked. One mode is teacherly:

Once when I was analyzing the symbolism of sun and moon in Coleridge's poem, "The Ancient Mariner," a student raised this objection: "I'm tired of hearing about the symbolic sun in poems, I want a poem that has the *real* sun in it."

Answer: If anybody ever turns up with a poem that has the real sun in it, you'd better be about ninety-three million miles away. We were having a hot summer as it was, and I certainly didn't want anyone bringing the real sun into the classroom.

Another is Prussian militarist cum Dr. Bovary. It appears in the few essays that address themselves (with an iron inattention to tone) to masterworks—the essay on "The Grecian Urn," for example, of which the following is the final paragraph:

We may contrast this discussion with explanations such as a materialist of the Kretschmer school might offer. I refer to accounts of motivation that might treat disease as cause and poem as effect. In such accounts, the disease would not be "passive," but wholly active; and what we have called the mental action would be wholly passive, hardly more than an epiphenomenon, a mere symptom of the disease quite as are the fever and the chill themselves. Such accounts would give us no conception of the essential matter here, the intense linguistic activity.

Another is perky-boyish-stubborn, as in Burke's replies to complainants like Hook and Blackmur. He will not "answer" these chiding parental voices; no concession that a brutal deed was done, only a reiteration that historical events are first of all changes in the way human beings choose to define themselves (innumerable choices are possible); no avowal that Miss Corelli is not Shakespeare, only an excursion on the inertness of the classifications of "good taste."

There have been occasions, true, on which this extraordinary contention against "natural" response, or openheartedness, is given over—the essay on "The Rhetoric of Hitler's 'Battle' " is a notable one. But by and large the critic is unrelentingly hostile to Normalcy. And in his latest and most self-regarding book, *The Rhetoric of Religion: Studies in Logolology,* Burke remains fiercely unsubmissive to the other writer's voice. The book opens, in the theorist's characteristic fashion, with trumpetry on the theme that words are not things ("Language, to be used properly, must be 'discounted' . . ."; "all words for the non-verbal must, by the very nature of the case, discuss the realm of the non-verbal in terms of what it is not"). Activizing as ever, it establishes that religion is a form of behavior, redefines behavior as verbal gesture, advances the proposition that "what we say about God will bear a likeness to what we say about words"—and justifies it with a swift clutch of analogies (God is to Christ as thought is to utterance; the succession of words in a sentence is to the meaning of a sentence as time is to Eternity). Thereafter the reader is offered an intense, lengthy, speculative Seeing Around of Augustine's *Confessions* and the opening chapters of Genesis, sections that conclude—on the basis of the grammar of the Biblical verses—that it is in the nature of language itself to construct "providence" or "divine foreknowledge" in principle: ". . . language is just made that way. And in its will is (our definition of) peace." The book ends with a dialogue that shoots off a thousand paradoxes on The Word, words, and conceptions of mystery, and there is enough brilliance in these pages, and twice as much wit, to support a thousand-acre seminary. But the unhearingness *is* muscularly resolute.

To repeat: the resoluteness is the key to the method. The critic never asked to be thought of as a man concerned with works of art "for themselves" or as "experiences" to be lovingly re-created; he never answered eloquence with eloquence.* He invariably asserts at the

---

* Burke possesses a high eloquence, but here as elsewhere it is released not by the other voice, but instead by one or another psycho-linguistic quirk that attracts his eye and tickles him into poetry—as in the following snippet: "Intimacy with a woman must always argue special intimacy with some word or words like or nearly like the sound of her name. So probably they [the

cruces—sometimes in ecstasy—the primacy of his interest ("Then comes what is, for our purposes, the most
astoundingly perfect passage conceivable"—this about a
moment in the *Confessions* that is, naturally, astounding
and perfect for many purposes besides those of the "comic"
perspectivist). Everything in his almost hostile manner
of address to the work announces **that** because it is a confession, a description, a vocabulary, a set of terms, it must
necessarily and inevitably be a deceit. Moreover: grounds
for forgiveness other than the man's frankness lie ready at
hand. Who, after all, would argue that Augustine's tale
of his conversion ought to convert a modern reader? Can
it really be said that the exasperation occasioned by
Burke's harping on Augustine the rhetorician ("an inveterate wordman" and "former word-merchant" occur on
page after page) is a major irritant? And is it not true
that the hunt for cues and buried symbols does eventually
come out at a trove? (The word-merchant's magnificent
passage on the union with God as unutterable silence is
shown convincingly to "tie in psychologically with motives
vestigially 'infantile.' ")

The questions are not easy to dismiss. But, confronting Burke in the context of general education, the reader
does tend to turn away from them—in the direction of the
obvious deeper problem. Taken to its end, bureaucratized,
brought the full way down into the arena to day-to-day,
might not the method easily be put in service of the cause
of moral laziness? You cannot *teach* caritas, sympathy,

names of Augustine's 'toys'] are there [in the *Confessions*] shining out like
unseen stars, ambiguously split between terms in the constellation of the
divine and terms for the problematic body."

respect for the other—but will these be strengthened if you teach their opposites? Discount the ideal and the labor of *recognition,* and how much of "the humanities" remains?

The possibility exists, needless to say, that intense imperviousness is simply part of the personal configuration called Kenneth Burke, rather than a telling mark and sign (among literary men) of the perspectivist disposition of mind. But examination of other writers of the school lends little backing to this theory. The most substantial recent work produced by a leading member is Stanley Edgar Hyman's *The Tangled Bank* (1962). The literary community owes many debts to this writer. His reviews are sharp, forceful, usually unsmutched by schmerz or phony brio. *The Armed Vision* has been a kind of sacred book for two generations of graduate students in English, strengthening their will to believe in the profession at just the moment when the latter presents itself most forcibly in the likeness of a poolshow. And in the new book mentioned, an important bureaucratization of the (Burkean) Imaginative, he has assembled invaluable materials for a perspectivist account of the development of the modern mind. But there is not much in the volume to suggest that imperviousness is a personal tic of the original (Burkean) genius.

As indicated by the subtitle—*Darwin, Marx, Frazer and Freud as Imaginative Writers*—Hyman is assessing the heroes of perspectivism: at last the revolution catches up, as it were, with the revolutionaries. To speak of him as a bureaucratizer of Burke is only to say that each of his chapters on the thinkers in question takes roughly the form of an attempt to specify, from a series of viewpoints, the proper rates of discount to be applied to their versions and visions of experience. The movement of the chapters is from biography through history into formal analysis. The characteristic gesture is of knitting contexts:

In reality, of course, Darwin's teleology is as sacred and supernatural as Paley's, but with all-seeing Mother Nature substituted for God the Father. It was a fit covert religious revolution for Victorian England, but it also had a particular fitness for Darwin, whose deep identification with his dead mother and submission to his overwhelming father suggests a classic Oedipal situation.

His [Darwin's] final moral imperative is curiously akin to Freud's concept of civilization as the taming of the instinctual life: 'The highest possible stage in moral culture is when we recognize that we ought to control our thoughts, and "not even in inmost thought to think again the sins that made the past so pleasant to us." ' The quotation is from *The Idylls of the King*. It shows as well as anything could . . . that *The Descent of Man,* this bold attack on Victorian orthodoxy, was the salvation of Victorian orthodoxy in the only terms, imaginative and poetic, in which it could still be saved.

The most obvious repression is of the instinct for reductive explanation; deflecting agents are ceaselessly renamed in multiplying contexts. (The tendency of Freud's work to "temporalize" belief in a "primal cause" into an origin myth must be placed not only in the context of Freud's guilt about his attachment to Fliess, but in the context of his imaginative fascination with the mode of Conan Doyle. Frazer's unclarity about the relations between history and myth, Christ the man and Christ the Saviour, must be placed in the context of contemporary religious argument—"he feels caught in the middle, a Straussite Unitarian fending off the Trinitarian worshippers in one direction and the Bauerite atheists on the other"; and also in the context of the uncertainty of his design—"perhaps the vastness of the book [*The Golden Bough*] really does break down.")* And the most interesting crisis traceable to the grand strategy takes the form of an Evaluative Situation, wherein the writer reprices back to list the object he has discounted—and then attempts to buy it off himself with a flourish.

An uneasy flourish, necessarily, because the discounter —using perspective by incongruity, analogical form, and a dozen other ploys—has driven hard bargains throughout. The "dramatic and tragic vision of life" in *The Descent of Man* "comes from Darwin, rather than from his subject matter." Frazer's "imaginative reconstruction of the performance of the mysteries in describing the great hall of Initiation of Eleusis seems to have more in common with the Radio City Music Hall than with anything that could have transpired at Eleusis. . . ." Freud's "fullest account of the bedevilled ego is a blare of metaphor." Neither Marx's nor anyone else's economic theories are "true or

---

* Hyman intends the word "temporalize" to bring Burke to mind here; in point of fact the observation about Freud's explaining present conditions by inventing a mythic past comes directly from *The Grammar of Motives* and *The Rhetoric of Religion*. On Hyman's *"Acknowledgments"* page Burke's name is placed third in a list of main influences (after the Cambridge School of anthropologists and Empson), and it appears only six times in the text. Burke's vocabulary, however, is used repeatedly, and his injunctions to commentators, historians, and critics are faithfully heeded; plainly but for him this book could not have been written.

false in any determinable sense." And *Capital* is best seen as:

> . . . a melodrama called something like *The Mortgage on Labor-Power Foreclosed.* In the first act the villain mistreats the virtuous wife and injures her poor little child; in the second act the young laboring hero himself is maimed and sits paralyzed in a wheelchair while the child dies; in the third act they are thrown out into the snow and take refuge in a miserable hovel; in the fourth act the discovery is made that the villain stole the mortgage originally and has no legal or moral rights over our heroes. It needs a fifth act in which the working-class family is rescued and restored to its happy home, but only the proletarian revolution could produce that final curtain, and Marx could not finish *Capital* without it.

But a return to Fair Trade is attempted, once the price-wearing is finished. The strategist begins his final chapter with abuse of those who have refused to take in the meaning (discounted? undiscounted?) of the writers he has been assessing:

> It is not that there has been a religious revival so much as an obscurantism revival, a disinterest in knowledge as a good in itself, perhaps a new failure of nerve. . . . The entrenched enemy that Darwin, Marx, Frazer and Freud each battled in his own fashion, the bigoted ignorance and superstition that masks as religion, has survived their onslaughts and is apparently stronger than ever.

He then sheds a seemingly disingenuous tear:

> Apart from the influence of religious obscurantism, our century generally seems less interested in ideas than the last, seems to care about them less and to take them less seriously.

Some of this is an unfortunate effect of the discounting Marx and Freud have taught us; it is so easy now to dismiss any idea as an ideology or a rationalization.

And thereafter, restoring metaphor as a value in an admirably bold stroke ("perhaps all science is ultimately metaphor, as Freud suggested in his open letter to Einstein"), he ends with a single powerful sentence of approbation: "These great enlightenings are humanist; philanthropic in the root sense, for the love of man."

The strategy of this closing is not without awkwardness, as the summary implies. But what is of interest is that the awkwardness plainly is traceable to the tendencies of mind under discussion here—ferocious resistance, stony imperviousness. Evidence in support of this point can be found in every section of Hyman's book, but particularly in the chapters on Marx and Engels. The latter pages are filled with observations on Marx's imaginative design, dramatic stance, and key metaphors (many of these are likely to seem puzzling to readers with a clear memory of *Capital* itself). But they are also dense with terms of another order—numbers, summaries of statistical tables, quotations from the reports of "firsthand observers" (of non-Marxist deflection) of the conditions of the working class. The reader is given information (originally supplied by Marx but not quarreled with by Hyman) about towns in which one of every four babies dies within a year of birth, about steel-pen and tile plants that employ children four and five years old, about class differences in life expectancy in cities like Liverpool and Manchester (fifteen years for workers, thirty-five years for the upper middle class), about tuberculosis rates (an increase of from one in forty-five to one in eight in a decade of lace-making), and about living space (eighteen people to a room in Newcastle). Only a page before the account of *Capital* as melodrama the writer repeats Marx's quotation from "a magistrate of the lace trade" on child labor:

Children of nine or ten years are dragged from their squalid beds at two, three, or four o'clock in the morning and compelled to work for a bare subsistence until ten, eleven, or twelve at night, their limbs wearing away, their frames dwindling, their faces whitening, and their humanity absolutely sinking into a stonelike torpor, utterly horrible to contemplate.

Against this language Hyman's heavy irony about a first act portraying a "villain [who] mistreats the virtuous wife and injures her poor little child" clanks incommensurately. The iron will to unresponsiveness has produced, on schedule, yet another analogical form—melodrama—but in meeting the schedule the author has revealed little except his terror of sounding like a bleeding heart. Embarrassed, the reader withdraws, distrusting any cause that requires him to see sweated children as metaphors.

If this tic, or tactlessness, appeared only once, concern about it could reasonably be belittled as finkery. But in truth it is never out of sight. A chapter or so after the cited passages, Hyman writes about the descriptions offered in Engels' *The Condition of the Working Class in England in 1844*—and distances them in similar fashion. He quotes Engels on the life of a working woman in Manchester:

M. H., twenty years old, has two children, the youngest a baby, that is tended by the other, a little older. The mother goes to the mill shortly after five o'clock in the morning, and comes home at eight at night; all day the milk pours from her breasts, so that her clothing drips with it—

and an account of the life of Sheffield laborers:

The cottages are old, dirty, and of the smallest sort, the streets uneven, fallen into ruts and in part without drains or pavement; masses of refuse, offal and sickening filth lie among standing pools in all directions, the atmosphere is poisoned by the effluvia from all these, and laden and darkened by the smoke of a dozen tall factory chimneys. A horde of ragged women and children swarm about here, as filthy as the swine that thrive upon the garbage heaps and in the puddles.

Then, faced with this sentence of his author:

Yet one is left in doubt whether even this terribly torturing death is not a blessing for the children in rescuing them from a long life of toil and wretchedness, rich in suffering and poor in enjoyment,

Hyman remarks: "When Engels falls into sentimentality, which is not infrequently, we may think of Dickens. . . . Engels [redoes] the death of Little Nell."

The question of moment is: what in the quoted sentence is sentimental? Where in the sentence are there feelings in excess of the value of the object? Why is the modern tongue incapable of saying that a sweated child is better off dead, is blessed in extinction? Admittedly the man who raises the question is obliged to suspect his own "interest": I am an opportunist eager to prove that the critic is a hard rock and I am sweet? I am a wailer big with hysterical cries?—as: The world is not words! the Jews were not

burnt in dictionaries! the past is not fiction! Frazer is not
Cecil B. DeMille! Something somewhere by someone *can*
be taken straight!—But after all the "necessary" self-
laceration the problem and the sensible conclusion still
stand forth in full sight. The problem is, simply, that the
last proud sentence of *The Tangled Bank*—". . . philanthropic in the root sense, for the love of man"—establishes that the author has fine feelings, but establishes it
later than might have been hoped. (Or, saying it again,
the hooks and eyes that connect the sentence—it occurs
450 pages deep in an oversized ten-dollar book—with
what has gone before have crept down under the facing and
are hard to reach.) And the conclusion is that the literary
perspectivist, for all his whirling, shifting agility, is finally
a man who does hate being moved.

In itself this conclusion is hardly an adequate basis for
an assessment of a complete teaching program—the program that features the viewpoints of Losing Coaches and
Eight Year Old Brothers. But from this it doesn't follow
that reading the school of Burke in the context of educational reform, scrutinizing it for hints as to the nature of
future gains and losses under the regime of the perspectivists, is an altogether improper act. (Such a reading does acknowledge the school's significance, after all,
even as it claims—in good Burkean fashion—that pedagogical revolutions themselves must not always be taken
on their own terms.) As for the losses: the thought of
them will turn no reasonable man into a counter-revolu-
tionary—for there are few alternatives to the regime.
Linguistic fundamentalism, as represented by the Rosicru-
cians and Boehme and the John Webster who didn't

write plays, is a pretty artifact, but vapid in its nostalgia for the old language of the old nature of the old Adam wherein every verbal sound contained the nature of the thing and no gap existed between verbal expression and reality. Linguistic progressivism from Leibnitz to the psycholinguists has its brisk utopian note, but also a constant overtone of kookieness. And the tough-minded objectivism of the short-haired ladies (Ayn Rand) and stern-browed men (Norman Mailer) is mainly dumb. You have only to shift your gaze from these items to Burke's beautifully complicated human landscape, or to Hyman's often admirably inclusive "history" to discover why the perspectivists are a modern center of hope.

The word to be said, in sum, *is* merely cautionary— meaning the word to be spoken to the humanist-perspectivist who is about to bring his vision out of the library and into the world of men, or of children. This enthusiast must tell himself that the future will be a place in which more will be seen or encompassed—every manifold stretching and stretching—every schoolboy peering over, through, around, underneath: for this is the way causes are made. But, even as he warms to the prospect, he needs to remind himself that the dilation of vision anticipated is more dependent upon the development of new perspectives, new languages, than upon the rigorous eschewal of the old; only if he does this will his cause escape reduction to technics. He must hear every word of the Burkemen: no perspective exempt from scrutiny, only multiplicity can be The Rock, the comic view is essential. And then as he repeats the lesson to youth he must corrupt it with gentleness: by choosing a tone expressive of the possibility that some acts of Seeing Around are more painful to witnesses than other acts, by implying that if imperviousness is the means, sympathy is the end, by contradicting those who think comic means A Joke, and by remembering, finally, that neither in mortuaries nor elsewhere is it demonstrable that wisdom and silence are the same.

1962

Acknowledgments

The author thanks Janet Aaron, Theodore Baird, Joseph Cady, Joel DeMott, Margaret DeMott, R. M. Douglas, Theodore Greene, Allen Guttmann, George Kateb, Leo Marx, James Ostendarp, William H. Pritchard, Herbert Spiro, R. C. Townsend, and John William Ward for generous help of many kinds.

3 1303 02014 8210

WITHDRAWN
FROM THE
PRATT INSTITUTE LIBRARY